Secrets of
Trout Fishing

Patrick Stephens Limited, part of Thorsons, a division of the Collins Publishing Group, has published authoritative, quality books for enthusiasts for more than twenty years. During that time the company has established a reputation as one of the world's leading publishers of books on aviation, maritime, military, model-making, motor cycling, motoring, motor racing, railway and railway modelling subjects. Readers or authors with suggestions for books they would like to see published are invited to write to: The Editorial Director, Patrick Stephens Limited, Thorsons Publishing Group, Wellingborough, Northants, NN8 2RQ.

Secrets of Trout Fishing

Roderick Wilkinson

PATRICK STEPHENS LIMITED

First published in 1990

British Library Cataloguing in Publication Data
Wilkinson, Roderick
    Secrets of Trout Fishing
    1. Trout. Angling
    I. Title
    799.1'755

ISBN 1-85260-253-8

Patrick Stephens Limited is part of the Thorsons Publishing Group, Wellingborough, Northamptonshire NN8 2RQ, England.

Printed in England by Woolnough Bookbinding Limited, Irthlingborough, Northamptonshire.
Typeset by MJL Limited, Hitchin, Hertfordshire.

10 9 8 7 6 5 4 3 2 1

Contents

Introduction

This book should begin, 'First take the fishing rod in your hand', because it is that kind of book — a simple step-by-step guide for those people who have always wanted to fish but have never been sure what to do, where to go, what to buy, or how to handle a fishing rod.

It has always been my impression, listening to would-be anglers, that they are more shy of the whole expertise and rigmarole than they will admit. 'I wouldn't have the patience', or 'I just don't have the time', or 'I have no idea where I can fish' — these are the kind of things I hear.

This book is intended to answer some of the questions that people want to ask about fishing — 'What do I buy?' 'Is it expensive?' 'Where do I start?' 'What do I put on the hook at the end of the line?' 'Is it like sea fishing?'

I make no excuse for over-simplification. Angling in all its facets — coarse fishing, sea angling, salmon angling, dry fly fishing, spinning — is complicated enough even for the experts, and I would only be adding to the complexity if I wrote about anything except the basic elements of a sport that is engrossing, healthy, challenging and fun. I would like to thank sincerely the good friends — angling experts and others — who helped me in producing the book and, more particularly, illustrating it with their pictures: Jim Kent, fishing tacklist in Glasgow, who supplied most of the items of equipment and clothing for the illustrations and posed for the casting positions; Granville Fox of Glasgow, who photographed them; John Walton, John Roberts and Bill Howes, specialist angling photographers, whose pictures also appear in the book; and Mrs Vera Brooks of Nottingham, who typed the script, and my long-suffering wife, who listened endlessly to my narration.

Chapter 1

Why take up fishing?

Statistics are usually a bore, but it must be said that in Britain fishing has over three million enthusiasts and is reckoned to be one of the fastest-growing, non-spectator sports in the world. More and more people are taking to the rivers and lakes, the shores and boats to test their skill in catching fish.

The fact that you have taken the time and trouble to pick up this book and read it proves something — you are attracted to the idea. I cannot tell why you feel you might want to fish, but I can support your notion with a few suggestions which may convert you to becoming one of these three million anglers.

Firstly, fishing is a fascinating sport that grows on you. It captivates you, makes you keenly interested because of the challenge. Don't think for a moment that catching fish is easy. Certainly some kinds of fish are easier to catch than others — for instance on certain days under certain conditions catching seafish like mackerel or codling can be relatively simple. But — and here's the odd thing about the sport — the simple catching of fish is *not* 'the name of the game'. I often feel that when anglers catch any type of fish too easily, they deliberately seek new ways of finding bigger ones, or more difficult ways of deceiving them. The spirit of competition is always there — in fishing hotels, where the day's lucky catch is displayed on the hall table, in clubs where there is constant striving for the prizes, and even among small groups that compare weights and sizes after a day's outing. But the main spirit of contest is felt by the angler between himself and the wily fish.

Secondly, it is a healthy sport. Angling takes you out into the open air on to a river bank or in a boat. More often than not it takes you to some wild, beautiful areas of the country where the atmosphere is a lung-filling benefit. You will be well exercised most of the time — perhaps walking for miles by a river, stalking your

prey, or rowing in a boat from one bay of a loch to the next. Even fishing from the bank on one of the many reservoirs and stillwaters that are available to anglers takes you into the open air and a healthy outdoor activity.

Third, compared with some other outdoor sports, fishing is not expensive — especially fishing for trout. A few pounds per day is the general outlay for a fishing permit on most waters. The equipment, as I will explain later, is not a heavy outlay. And in Britain at any rate, fishing waters can be reached in an hour or less from most cities and towns. Areas further afield can be reserved for holidays.

I am not suggesting for a moment that an angler will find it difficult to spend a lot of money on his sport, especially if he insists, later in his sporting life, on buying expensive rods and reels and equipment, and is determined to rent one of those

Left *Fly fishing on the River Test near Romsey.*

Left *Two ways of fishing a lake — from boat or bank.*

Right *There is no sex discrimination in angling — as this lucky lady shows.*

highly priced salmon beats that can run to hundreds of pounds for a week, or to travel great distances to foreign waters.

I am writing this piece for the ordinary would-be angler who wants to start off modestly, learn the skill step by step and 'crawl before he runs'. If you are one of those, be assured that the sport need cost you very little.

Like golf, fishing is a sport that suits men and women, boys and girls, old people, young people. Bear this in mind — the fish have no idea at all who is at the other end of the rod. They don't care if the angler is an absolute beginner or an expert. Fishing lore is filled with tales of the most unusual people catching the most surprising number or size of fish. Indeed, beginners are usually very lucky, simply because they are not complacent or idle. They keep at it until something happens.

Angling is a sport, too, that attracts different personalities. If you are a gregarious person who likes good company and plenty of chit-chat and cheerful companions, you will find all of that in a fishing club that has regular outings. On the other hand, if you prefer your own company, there are miles of rivers and waters in beautiful surroundings waiting to give you all the solitude you want. Your family? Yes, there are always opportunities for you to take your spouse and your children on a day's outing, or on a longer fishing holiday. Those who do not wish to fish can do plenty of other things while you fish. It *can* be very much a 'together' sport.

What I am advising you to do, therefore, if you feel you would like to be an angler, is take up trout fishing — at least for starters. The trout is a cunning, clever adversary. Catching him is a good challenge. And he inhabits the rivers and lakes that are easy enough for you to reach.

But why trout fishing?

With all the species of fish swimming in rivers and lakes and the sea around the coasts, and with all the different kinds of angling available to a beginner, why would he (or she) want to take up *trout* fishing? Salmon are bigger, more valuable, and are recognized as the king of fish. Coarse fish are probably more plentiful than game fish — at any rate more people fish for them in Britain. And the ocean is simply teeming with cod, haddock, flounders, wrasse, bass and scores of other fish ready to give the fisherman good sport either from the shore or the boat. Again, more people fish for them than for game fish. So why take up trout fishing?

Well, first and foremost it is a matter of individual choice (to say nothing of taste). But there surely *must* be something special about this particular fish, which has encouraged anglers and writers to extol its magnificence as a sporting fish for hundreds of years.

I can only give you my own version of the enthusiasm, based on years of fishing for this splendid fish. I have fished for coarse fish, sea fish, salmon and seatrout, but I can only say that it is the brown trout that has given me the most pleasure. It comforts me to know that I am not alone in this affection (or affliction). Next time you visit your local library, take a look along the 'angling' bookshelf and count the number of books devoted to trout fishing versus any other kind of fish.

What I like about angling for trout above anything is that it is a difficult fish to catch: it seems to be predictable in its haunts

Right *A pound brown trout from a Yorkshire stream.*

Below *The brown trout waits behind boulders for its food to float down the river to him.*

and feeding habits, yet just when you think you have him 'to rights', he starts feeding on something you are not offering; just when you think you know where he is bound to be lying, he has darted off somewhere else; just when you think the weather or the season is ideal for offering him an artificial fly to match the real thing, he decides to feed on something else. And — most important — just when you think you have caught him, he spits out your fly and is off.

There is another attraction, too, about fishing for trout which really has little to do with the fish itself — and that's his habitat. In most places, most of the time, the brown trout lives in beautiful waters — browsing behind rocks on sunny afternoons in moorland streams, cooling himself on hot days in the white water of a tumbling mountain river, lurking in the depths of wide Highland lochs, feeding cautiously among the wafting weeds of southern chalk streams, or browsing just offshore in one of the many reservoirs now stocked with fish. The trout belongs to the best of our country waters, and seeking him out takes the angler into some of our most beautiful countryside.

There are many species of fish which can be referred to as 'trout'. For example, the seatrout is a type of trout which comes in from the sea to spawn — like the salmon — in the fresh water of our rivers. Then it goes back out to sea. Although his cousin, the brown trout is a resident of the river and does not go to sea at all, we do have in Britain a kind of estuary trout (sometimes called a 'slob trout') which is pink-fleshed but travels no further than the brackish water of a river-mouth.

The three main kinds of trout which you are likely to catch (in Britain at any rate) are the brown trout (*Salmo trutta*), the rainbow trout (*Salmo gairdneri*) and the American brook trout (*Salvelinus fontinalis*). There are other kinds, of course, for example the Gileroo trout, but in the main these three mentioned are the most familiar. Incidentally, for legal purposes, the migrating seatrout is considered the same as salmon.

The brown trout breeds well in rivers and certain lochs — particularly in Scotland, Wales and Ireland — and is slow growing and lives long. It can grow to a weight of twenty pounds over about ten years.

It is very territorial in its habits, likes to feed in the same areas of water, breeds during autumn and winter in the little burns and

Left *Angling veteran Bill Howes with an 8lb rainbow trout caught from the bank of a lake.*

Right *Fisherman on the bank of Tunstalk Reservoir in Weardale.*

tributaries, then it is at its best for angling from May till September. It is often reared in hatcheries for restocking lakes, reservoirs and rivers.

The rainbow trout is a slightly different sort of fish. It was first introduced to Britain from Western USA in about 1884, and is now artificially reared and stocked. It grows fast and has been known to reach weights over 20 lb. After restocking in a river or lake, the rainbow tends to feed in shoals. It is generally hardier than the brown trout and it can withstand high temperatures and low oxygen levels.

The American brook trout thrives best in deep, cold water. It came originally from Eastern USA, and it too grows fast, but does not attain the weight of the other two types. Five or six pounds is about the limit. However, it is a strong fighter.

For the angler, there are many advantages to fishing for rainbows. They are more prone to rise than brown trout, and they are far more active in their search for food, going to the bottom then rising to the surface fairly continuously. Sometimes they can be as predatory as pike, and in waters where there are roach, they sometimes moves in 'hunting packs', driving shoals of small fish into the shallow waters, where they can beat them down savagely. Perhaps this is why lure-fishing on lakes for rainbow can be so

successful.

Wildlife and the quiet serenity of open spaces, we share much of the time with the trout. Angling for him brings us a constant challenge, a contemplative turn of mind, peace, and the 'joy of the chase'.

In a typical fishing water, you don't fish for trout so much as stalk him. Sooner or later you will get to know how to recognize where he is feeding — or even where he *should* be feeding. You will know where to present your artificial fly or your bait to deceive him. And he will deceive you just as readily. If the sun is on your back and your long shadow in a evening falls over where he is lurking, be sure he will be off. If you step noisily into the water, don't expect him to remain where you saw him.

So much for choice. Your taste is something else. But the person who doesn't like a well-prepared, well-cooked brown trout is a rarity. It is a nourishing, delectable dish. Indeed, I prefer it to salmon or cod or haddock.

The growth in fishing for trout has been quite phenomenal in Britain. In 1960 the government mandated the various water authorities to open their reservoirs to the public, and from then the whole activity has boomed. Private trout fisheries joined this explosion of the sport, which was more pronounced in the Midlands and south of England simply because of the previous shortage of game fishing opportunities at moderate cost in those areas. More and more coarse fishers who once angled for carp and tench and roach changed to descend on the 'new' reservoirs and lakes in thousands, to fish for both brown and rainbow trout.

Some myths exploded

Before you think about taking up trout fishing as a hobby, there are a few myths about the sport, which I would like to explode. And the first of these is that it is a lazy person's activity.

Even though fishing is an outdoor activity, some people liken it to snooker or bridge or darts — good fun, and mentally stimulating in a way, but hardly a 'sport', and certainly not calling for much physical effort.

You can hardly blame non-anglers who think this way. The reason is mainly statistical — in Britain, at any rate. There are three and a half million anglers in this country, roughly half of whom are coarse fishers who catch the uneatable, retain them under water in keep-nets, then put them back into the river or lake after the 'weigh-in'. Of the remaining half of the total, a quarter are sea anglers who fish from rocks or out in boats around the coast. This leaves the remaining quarter which consists of game fishers — that is, anglers who fish for salmon, seatrout or trout. In round figures that's about one hundred thousand. Take away the salmon fishers and you have around eighty thousand.

Now where do you imagine most people get the idea that fishing — that is, any kind of fishing — is an inactive pastime? How do they get the picture in their minds of a line of anglers along a river bank, each one seated on a little chair or on a wicker hamper under an umbrella, his rod fixed on the bank and his line with a float on it out in the water as he waits hour after hour for a bite? Some even have a little bell to signal a bite.

Look at the statistics again and you will see the answer. Half the anglers in Britain fish this way. The trout anglers — fly fishers mostly — are very much a minority, which is why they tend to be merged in people's minds with the coarse fishers under their umbrellas.

The second myth, ironically, is one which seems to contradict the first one — that it is a 'chuck-it-and-chance-it' kind of sport which requires the minimum of skill and the maximum of good luck.

Luck, of course, *is* one of the necessary ingredients, just as it is to a greater or lesser degree in hang-gliding, arctic exploration or boxing. An unlucky trout angler is roughly in the same category of destiny as an unlucky rock climber, except that one loses fish and the other might lose his life. Apart from the vagaries of fate, however, I have no hesitation in saying that fishing for trout is something more than a sport. It is an art, a science, a

John Walton fishing for the wild brown trout of Upper Teesdale.

philosophy, a way of life, a lifetime's study.

In no other sport will you find such wide-ranging interests in other aspects of nature, as in fishing. Entomology and the study of insect life is only the start of the angler's studies. His observations on the flora and fauna of the waterside are chronicled every month as literary by-products of this mainstream hobby — the angling magazines and books give plenty of evidence of this, from the earliest times of Izaak Walton. The trout's breeding and feeding habits and day-by-day routine through the seasons of the year have been the subject for hundreds of angling writers.

Yes, there is a small element of luck about fly fishing for trout. But those who view it with disdain for this reason have never seen the dry-fly angler painstakingly fashion and tie his own flies, absolute replicas of the real insects he has gathered in his small butterfly net from above the surface of the water. Nor has he overheard the earnest talk in the fishing tacklists shop about nylon breaking-strains, hook sizes, rod weights, line specifications, dimensions of flies — to say nothing of wind direction, water temperature and where the fish may lie.

There is another myth about fishing for trout, which really deserves much more attention from non-angling doctors than it gets — and that is the belief that it is not an 'open-air exercise'

Dry fly fishing on a Yorkshire stream.

kind of sport.

That it is an 'open-air' activity is not in question. What these non-fishing medical advisers don't seem to realize is that the trout fisher *stalks* his quarry, as does a hunter. This means that he is constantly on the move along a river bank or a lakeside, until he finds a spot which will be his arena, his tournament place where he will cast his flies time after time, exploring with them every likely nook and cranny of the water where a fish may be lurking. The 'no exercise' critics have evidently never spent a whole day casting a dry fly on a river, avoiding the drag of the nylon leader, raising the rod, gathering line — then casting again and again before moving on, climbing over rocks, tramping along the bank, and wading into another pool to repeat the whole process.

You only have to look at bank fishers on a reservoir or a lake long-lining in their search for a trout to realize that shooting-head lines, or those with forward tapers, were not manufactured for the feeble-armed or those who do not like physical effort. Heaving these lines with their lures on the end out thirty yards or so then hand-hauling them back with dexterity time after time is not for the haters of exercise.

And fishing from a boat? I make the same defence. Hour after hour of loch-style surface casting or long-lining is strenuous, enjoyable and, of course, wildly exciting when a fish is taken. I need hardly mention the physical benefits of rowing, too, in those stillwaters where outboard engines are not allowed.

I make no case for trout fishing being in the same beneficial category of exercise as running or gymnastics. All I am saying is that it is *not* a spectator sport!

Chapter 2

Gearing up

What you need

Obviously you must have a rod — let's look at that first. Fishing rods come in all lengths, types, materials and prices. Over the past fifty years they have progressed from split-cane rods, then fibreglass rods and on to the present enthusiasm for carbon-fibre and boron-fibre rods.

I make no particular recommendation as to the material of the rod. Certainly split-cane is the traditional type, and still used enthusiastically by anglers who would never dream of using fibre rods. Fibreglass rods are usually cheaper, light to handle and almost unbreakable. Carbon-fibre rods are lighter still, but a little more expensive.

Regardless of the type or price you choose, I would suggest you need a rod of 9 feet to 10 feet for wet-fly fishing for trout.

What is important is that you buy a good rod — one with an established maker's name on it. Take the advice of the fishing tackle dealer, and whatever else you may wish to save on, don't penny-pinch on the rod. It is to be your most important fishing friend for many years.

There are now many schools for casting, all over the country, and it would be a good idea to join one of these for a few lessons before you buy a rod at all. Then, based on the advice of a qualified instructor, you will be able to buy the rod best suited to you.

Never forget that if you buy the wrong kind of rod or, worse still, simply 'inherit' one that has no relevance to you, it is quite possible for you to develop bad casting habits right at the beginning, which may never leave you and may inhibit your sport ever after. Start as you mean to finish — competently.

Next, you will need a reel, and here I am not so fastidious.

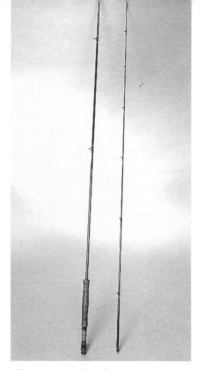

Choose a good rod.

The wrong rod can cause bad casting habits.

Most good trout-fishing reels will serve you very well.

There is, however, a reel on the market which is automatic in its retrieval of the line. There is a spring device operated by a small lever which can be touched by the little finger, and the line will retrieve on to the spool very fast. This type of reel is favoured by some dry-fly anglers and by those reservoir fishers who throw long casts, then retrieve their lines quickly.

A rod with the sliding ring and the screw ring.

Although this kind of reel looks and sounds from its description to be a 'wonder tool', frankly I would not recommend it for a beginner. The simpler the better is the maxim for him.

One of the most frustrating things that can happen to an angler is for his reel to come apart from the rod. This usually happens, ironically, when he is playing a fish. The reason is always the same — the reel is insecurely fastened to the rod.

The reel should fit tightly into the rod, so that it will not pull off. The beginner would be well advised to check this from time to time when fishing. Discovering it loose when playing a fish is too late.

Sliding rings are one way of fastening the reed to the rod, and many manufacturers still use these, although my preference is for the screw reel fitting. Where there are two screw nuts on this type, the bottom one should be checked for tightness at least once when on the water.

Reels should be well taken care of, by cleaning and the application of a little oil occasionally.

There are many, many different brands and kinds of line on the market. Quite apart from the reputation or otherwise of the makers, what the fishing tacklist cannot guess is where and how you intend spending most of your fishing days. On a river? Up at the local reservoir (here he can be of valuable assistance)? On a loch many miles away? From a boat? From the bank?

His job in helping you is not easy. There are floating lines, sinking lines, fast sinkers, slow sinkers, weight-forward lines, shooting-head lines, lead-covered ones and lines with sinking tips.

There *is* one thing you can do to help make a decision. Go to the water where you feel you may be doing most of your fishing, at least at the beginning of your fishing life. It may be a nearby river or a reservoir, or a private fishing lake. Walk along the bank and talk to those anglers who are resting. (Don't, under any circumstances, try to talk to one who is fishing — he may eat you!) Ask him what type of line he is using. Ask him why. Then ask him to give you a brief demonstration.

Armed with this knowledge you are in a better position now to discuss the question of lines with the fishing tacklist, and make your choice.

Just above the handle of your rod you will probably see a figure. The purpose of this AFTM number (Association of Fishing Tackle Manufacturers) is to show you the size of line most suitable for the rod. If you take care with this matching of rod and line, you will find casting easier, more competent and less tiring during a fishing day.

Not everything that is on a reel, however, is line. The line itself

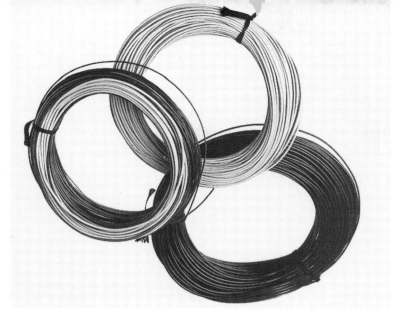

Three types of line — floater, sinker and sinking tip.

may only be about 30 yards long, so why does the drum look so well stacked with line right up to about an eighth of an inch from the rim? The answer to this is the backing. This is a length of non-operative line which goes on to the drum first so that the reel is well stacked. Otherwise your 30 yards of line would be too puny and difficult for casting.

The figures on the rod indicates the most suitable line to be used.

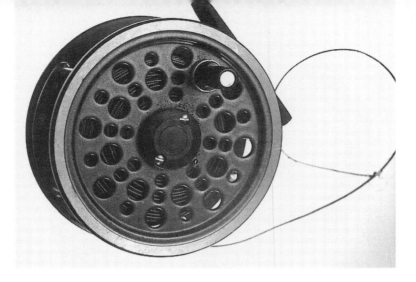

The fly line is one of the three links between you and the fish. One of its main features is that it must be of sufficient weight to flex the rod when you are casting. The code letters used by the manufacturers are:

D T   Double taper
W F   Weight forward
S   Sinking
F   Floating

A double-tapered line is made with the line tapering from the middle, becoming slimmer and slimmer to each end of the line.

The 'weight forward' line is used in long-distance casting, usually on a lake. And the sinking and floating lines are obvious in their purpose.

Colour of line is a matter of individual taste and judgement. Some anglers prefer one colour, others another, but as a general rule a light colour is preferable for floating line, simply because you can see it on the water when you cast.

A fly line is usually about 30 yards long, and they are made in different weights. For instance the AFTM number 4 or 5 is about right for dry-fly fishing on a calm day but where there's a hefty wind, No.6 suits better. In wet-fly fishing where you are casting a long line, No.8 or 9 would be better. A fast-sinking line once it reaches the water will sink at a rate of six inches per second.

Now we come to the cast (the Americans call it the leader), which is the length of nylon fixed at the end of your line and on which you will be tying your artificial flies that will deceive the trout. Never forget that this length of nylon is the weakest link in your 'chain' to the fish. Nylon casts come two ways. Most fishing tackle shops sell made-up casts all ready for you to tie on to the end of your line. A cast for wet-fly fishing usually carries three

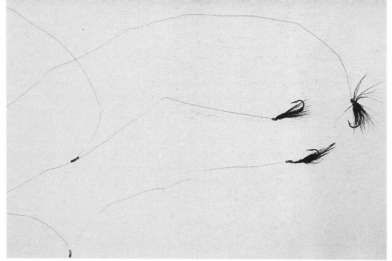

Above left *A well-packed reel ready for action.*

Above *A cast for wet fly fishing usually has three artificial flies.*

Right *The best kind of leader for dry fly fishing is a knotless taper.*

artificial flies — one hanging down near where the nylon is tied on to your line, one hanging down in the middle of the cast, and one at the very end, called the tail-fly. And the ready-made cast is indeed all ready for you to tie on your flies.

For dry-fly fishing — that is fishing with a single artificial fly — the best kind of leader to buy is a knotless taper. This type of cast is excellent for the dry-fly angler, but there is one snag. Dry-fly fishing often means changing flies frequently, and every time there is a change it means another little length coming off the leader. Sooner or later you will be left with a shortened leader, the bottom part of which is now around 6 lb breaking strain whereas it started off as one of 4 lb.

Most dry-fly anglers prefer to make up their own leader using three different thicknesses of nylon, tying each one with a blood knot so that the entire cast is in the form of a taper.

For wet-fly fishing — and this is what I recommend for the novice as a starting method — you can buy a knotless tapered leader with two droppers. This can be an excellent choice for either river or lake fishing.

If you intend making up your own casts, what breaking strain of nylon should you buy? Well, for a start, I would suggest that your total length of leader should be nine feet. You will find this easy to handle and, most importantly, the knot to your fly line will not catch in passing through the top ring of your rod. Many a good fish has been lost when this has happened.

You might make up your nylon leader in the following ratio:

    4 feet of 12 lb breaking strain, followed by
    3 feet of 8 lb breaking strain, then
    2 feet of 6 lb breaking strain.

Most anglers, however, prefer to make up their own casts, and for this purpose you buy a complete reel of, say, 200 yards of nylon of the appropriate breaking strain. What is breaking strain? Well, that depends on the size of fish you hope to catch, but since the most common size of trout you are likely to hook on a river will be anything between half-a-pound and three pounds, a relatively light breaking-strain nylon of five or six pounds should put you in no danger of the fish snapping off your cast. What you must remember, of course, is that a fish of one pound weight, in its acrobatics when hooked can exert a strain much greater than its

You will need a folding net.

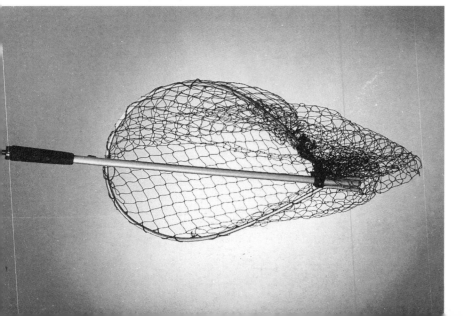

own weight. One way or another, that is the compromise — the deception of the fish balanced against the breaking strain of the nylon.

Now you need a net — a folding one, I suggest, because it is less cumbersome — and a small side haversack. Let's consider this haversack for a moment, which will be slung over your shoulder and carried resting on your hip.

This is for carrying all the small pieces of equipment you may need — fly box, casts, spare reel, scissors etc., and possibly your vacuum flask and your sandwiches for lunch. It is not for carrying fish.

There was a time when trout anglers — especially those on rivers — had a fish creel slung over their shoulder. This was a small wicker basket with a slot on the top, though which they shot the trout they caught. It was a fish-carrier — nothing more — and it was usual to have any number of fish, from two to twenty, each weighing three-quarters of a pound.

In today's terms, such a carrier would be quite redundant. Most trout anglers now fish in stillwaters, either from the bank or out in boats, and many of these stillwaters hold both brown trout and rainbows of considerable weights. Ten or fifteen pounders are not uncommon, and the idea of taking monsters like these home in a creel is quite impractical — and this is one of the reasons why it is no longer in use by anglers.

The ideal fish-carrier for today's stillwater trout angler is a bass

. . .and a small haversack is NOT for carrying fish.

Left *An angler's waistcoat.*

Above *A hat is essential for protection*

Below right *Thigh-length waders with studded or felt soles.*

bag, which is simply a canvas holdall with handles. It retains the catch — even the biggest fish — and keeps it fresh. Then the bass bag can be washed out easily.

You may be tempted into buying one of those angler's waistcoats with pockets for everything — scissors, casts, flies, weights etc. — and I certainly recommend it, although if I were just starting the sport I would be inclined to wait a while.

There is an old saying 'you'll never catch a fish unless you're wearing a funny hat'. That may be true but more seriously a fishing hat is essential for protection against other anglers' misplaced casts and, of course, against the weather — sunshine or rain.

The last thing I would mention as a necessity is a pair of thigh-length waders. Preferably they should have studded or felt soles (rubber soles may cause you to slip on rocks or the river bed) and they should be chosen of the right size with care as you may be wearing them all day. When not in use, the waders should be hung up feet-first to air and dry. You can buy metal grips for hanging waders up.

Buying the gear that is best for you

It is usually about mid-way through the afternoon on a day's fishing outing that you will know whether you have a properly balanced rod, reel and line. And if your arm is tired, if you feel ill-at-ease casting, or if you just can't 'feel right' every time you put those flies on the water — it is then you will wish you had paid more attention to the fishing tackle dealer's advice. Nothing is worse than an ill-balanced rod, reel and line.

These three things — rod, reel and line — should feel as though they are part of your arm. Casting out flies should be a very 'easy' rhythmic motion, once you have mastered the technique. The rod-maker's art over the years, both in split cane and fibre, has improved steadily, so that it is quite possible now to buy a rod that weighs only four ounces and can be used all day without strain.

A too-heavy reel, of course, can negate all the advantages of a light rod. So can a line that is too heavy. For these reasons, time spent with the tackle dealer getting the balance right is seldom wasted. Trying out a rod briefly in the shop itself is not a good enough test. You should ask to try it out in his back-yard if he has one, or in some other open space where you can use the rod,

Above *This angler is side-casting to place his flies correctly.*

Left *When not in use the waders should be hung up to dry.*

Right *You can make up your own fly box.*

reel and line time after time until you are quite sure it is the right tackle for you.

A 'balanced' tackle means what it says — when rod, reel, line and leader are all working in harmony when fly fishing. It is really the choice of the rod which governs the selection of the rest of the tackle; this is why I recommend that the greatest care possible should be taken before buying one. Whatever else you might want to save money on, don't let it be the rod.

The AFTM ratings marked on rods and on the packages containing any line you buy are your sure guide to balanced equipment. Although today's carbon-fibre rods are remarkably tolerant of mismatched lines with rods, there is a limit to their endurance. A line must be of the correct weight to flex the rod. If the line is too light it will cause you to cast clumsily. If it is too heavy it overloads the rod, and casting can be awful. It has been known for a rod to break with a line which is too heavy.

There is usually a temptation, too, to buy thigh-length waders too quickly, without paying attention to how they feel after hours on a river. The fact that they are leak-proof is probably the most obvious asset — hardly worth checking for in waders from a reputable maker. What *is* important is how they fit. Try them on — both legs. Walk up and down in them. See how securely they fasten. Stamp your feet and make sure they don't chafe because they are half a size too big; make sure they don't pinch because they are a fraction too small. If in doubt, buy them elsewhere. Uncomfortable waders which either nip your toes or flop about your heels can ruin your day's fishing. Remember, you may want to wear two pairs of socks to keep out the cold; allow for that when you try them on.

The gadgetry

This list of small items is what I call the gadgetry. I do not mean to trivialize these things, but they are desirable additions to the angler's kit.

Fly box
Don't keep your loose flies anywhere except in a fly box. It is safer and helps to prevent the hooks rusting. Buy a small box, because this will limit the selection of flies you buy and, for a beginner, this is a good thing.

If you feel like it you can make your own fly box, as I do. I buy an empty video box — the plastic kind in which videos are normally kept — and I cut sections of foam plastic and fit them inside. Then I simply fix my flies in order of size on to the plastic foam.

Scissors

Don't use your teeth to sever nylon. And don't use a knife. Use scissors or, if you prefer it, a nail clipper. You can buy fisherman's scissors these days, with pliers at the tips of the blades.

Priest

This is a small baton made of wood or horn with a lead core, which is used, as the name suggests, for administering the 'last rites' to the fish when you catch him. Never leave a fish gasping on the river bank or in a boat. Despatch it as quickly and humanely as possible with a couple of sharp blows on the head with the priest.

Puncture repair outfit

Get this in a cycle shop. You may be glad of it if your waders spring a leak and you have to do a repair on the spot, on the river bank.

Hook sharpener

You can buy these little grooved sharpeners now for use if and when your hooks lose their edge.

Scissors, a priest and a hook sharpener.

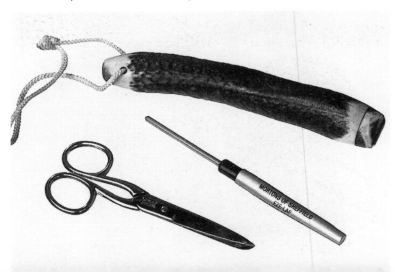

Sunglasses

Strong sunshine dappling on the surface of the water can cause eyestrain and detract from your hunting for signs of rising trout. Buy polaroids, which will cut the surface glare and make your fishing more comfortable.

Marrow spoon

This is a long spoon with no wide part at the end like an ordinary spoon. Its purpose is to find out what the trout has been feeding on. You insert the spoon through its mouth and 'spoon' out the contents of its stomach. Then you examine these contents to see the type of insect it has been eating so that you can match them with your artificial flies or nymphs.

Weights

Buy a box of small *non*-lead weights, in case you may be fishing a lake and you want to get your flies right down to the fish.

Torch

You may be glad of this one warm summer evening fishing in the sunset when trying to find your way back to your car in darkness.

Your clothing

Unlike some other outdoor sports, the clothing for angling, as a rule, is inexpensive and simple.

Sunglasses, a marrow spoon and a box of weights.

A waterproof coat should be long enough to cover the top of your waders.

Coat

Don't buy a plastic waterproof. Certainly it will keep the rain off, but it will not keep you dry simply because it develops condensation inside.

Buy a coat that is long enough to go over the top of your waders. The modern waxed cotton coats are excellent and there is a wide variety of quality and prices at the tacklist's shop. You get what you pay for.

Hat

A good fishing hat with a wide brim is invaluable on a fishing day. It shields the eyes from the sun, protects your head from the rain and — most importantly — it protects you from artificial flies when you and others are casting.

Gloves

I never wear them, even on the coldest days, but what I do recommend for the icy weather is a pair of fingerless mittens.

Socks

A spare pair of warm socks can be a blessing if you slip and fill your waders.

Braces

The Americans call them 'suspenders', and they are necessary for holding up your thigh-length waders.

Whatever clothing you buy, make sure it is not of bright lurid colouring. Merge with the background and the fish will not be 'spooked' off.

Chapter 3

The quarry

The trout season

The season in the UK is from 15 March to 6 October, although many fishing owners and managers — especially on lakes and reservoirs in the south — are extending the season right on into late October or November. In the case of rainbow trout, there is no close season at all. Before you set off to fish, therefore, you should check the dates of the opening and closing of the season on the particular water.

What is the best month for fishing for trout? Well, that depends on many things, but mainly geography. In general terms, in Britain the further north you go, the later the season for the best trout fishing. Climate, environment, plant growth and insect life have all to do with this, and just as in the northern parts of Britain plants and flowers come to bloom later than in the south, similarly trout come to 'bloom' later, too.

For all this, some rivers like the Don in Aberdeenshire have some excellent early spring trout; a lot depends on the feeding habits and the surroundings which produce this feeding.

Let us assume, however, that you want to fish sometime between May and August. What is more important is for you to know when and under what conditions you will stand a chance of catching trout. Again, this varies from place to place and water to water, but, working on the basis of my own experience, here are the times I favour:

- In spring and early summer, trouting is at its best in daytime — especially in the rough water and ends of runs where the lively fish are feeding on passing flies etc.
- As summer progresses, they tend to drift in towards the bank and under stones, hiding as it were, and it is usually in the

early morning or in the evening that they are at their best.

- By midsummer, night fishing is superb on many waters. The bigger fish tend to come out and feed fearlessly, and you can have marvellous fishing in the violet half-light of a summer night, with a short recess from midnight till first light. Usually bigger flies should be used then.
- In midsummer you will find excellent trout rising for flies at sunset or in the early light of dawn. Beginner or not, don't try night fishing on a strange stretch of river which you have not examined thoroughly beforehand.
- Midsummer or not, if conditions are good and there is plenty of water in the river (but not in spate) the best trout are usually there at the ends of runs or at the very ends of the pools. Remember that fish feed by facing *upstream*.
- As darkness creeps in, the fish, usually the larger ones, move down to the tail-ends of the pools, where they feel safe.
- Imagine yourself to be a trout. Where would *you* lie? Wouldn't you feed where the water seems to bring the insects to you? And wouldn't you lie near a rock or bank so that when danger threatens you could comfortably hide and keep concealed with the minimum of effort? Well, that's what the trout will do.

A dragonfly on a fishing rod handle.

How and where the trout feeds

You should understand something about how the trout feeds and what it eats in the river or the lake.

Up until they reach a certain size, trout feed on insects and other small water creatures. Then when they reach a size which these creatures can no longer nourish, the trout turns cannibal and will eat other smaller fish — even small trout.

Except in very cold weather, trout will rise to the surface to snatch insects and when they do, this is called a 'rise'. So you know what he means when an angler is sitting on a river bank and says he is 'waiting for the rise'. In warmer weather, trout feed most of the time from the surface. In a river the insects are carried downstream to the fish, which usually lie at a suitable spot to get them. This spot is called the 'lie'.

The trout is predatory. It will 'have a go' at a fly or bug or insect or other living creature in or on the water. It is a fish which selects its food according to the season and, quite naturally, takes what it can get to provide it with the most energy for the least effort. As the various insects and other water creatures vary their cycle of life, so the trout will change its own feeding habits.

As winter becomes spring, the trout are mainly bottom feeders on snails, beetles, shrimps etc. Then as summer approaches they feed on the increasing fly life on and below the surface as insects mate, descend, hatch eggs then die. At all stages of the life of mayflies, sedge and stone flies, the trout will feed on them. This continues right through summer, when more land flies are blown on the water and join the menu. Then as autumn progresses and the water temperature falls, the trout return to bottom feeding, until at below five degrees centigrade they stop feeding and remain this way through winter.

One of the reasons why the fishing season for rainbow trout can start earlier is simply because these fish start feeding earlier and will carry on later, cold or no cold.

The flies you use for angling are supposed to match those on which the trout is feeding at that moment in time. This is what makes the whole business of selecting the correct pattern and size of fly so intriguing.

The trout is interested in its survival, which means three things — its shelter, its food and its reproduction. The place where you are most likely to find the fish in a river or a lake, is where *you* might be if you were a trout.

So far as food is concerned, look for insects on the water or on the surface and watch for any tell-tale rings which show where a trout is feeding on these. If there is no activity on the surface of the water, fish around weedbeds or rocks, or where the water runs under banks — that is where the bottom-feeders are hunting for snails or larvae or minnows. In a river, much of the insect life is swept in backwaters, away from the main current. In a lake or reservoir it usually gets blown by the wind on to the lee shore.

When looking for likely places where trout might lie, the task is somehow easier on a river. Where would *you* be if you wanted shelter and safety? That's where the trout will be — under banks, in deep holes, behind large rocks, thus sheltering from the force of the current. They are never far away from their feeding areas, so that as dusk comes and the light is fading they can move in safety out to the current and feed on the insects coming downriver.

Fortunately for anglers, trout are fairly predictable in their feeding habits. This means that a beginner can train himself to use his eyes and look for the spots where he is most likely to catch a fish — *and*, of course, the tell-tale rings on the water which reveal a feeding fish.

It is difficult to offer precise guidance about where trout might be lying in a specific river but, based on my own experience, here are a few hints which will help to simplify the search.

- Once you know that you are on a trout river, go to the nearest bridge and look down into the water through polaroid glasses — preferably on a good, clear day or evening. Keep staring into the water and, if you are lucky, you'll see a trout. See how he remains almost motionless behind a rock or weeds or close to the bank, only the languid, gentle movements of his tail keeping him in the one position. Then watch him as he moves rapidly but smoothly out and up to the surface to take a passing insect. There is a ring on the water, that's all. Then he resumes his vigilant posture facing upstream.

- On warm days, and particularly in early summer, trout tend to go where the water is well aerated, and this means the rough 'white' water. There they can shelter behind rocks and snatch passing food. This kind of place often holds the larger fish.

- When the water is low, however, and the weather warm in summer, many of the decent-size fish keep under the banks out of sight and emerge only at dusk to feed. Indeed, when the sun is going over the horizon that's when you'll see them feeding in the smooth water and at the very ends of pools.

- Thundery weather keeps the trout out of sight, they will not be interested in flies.

- When the river is running in spate and is yellow or brown, they are not interested in fly life because they are getting worms, etc. from the spate.

- Very cold weather also discourages them from feeding on flies — probably because flies are very scarce anyway in low temperatures.

In lakes the trout rest at certain times of the day in sheltered places, then when conditions are right, they move out and cruise about to feed on flies. The 'right' conditions are like those on rivers, when the light is fading or when there is a good breeze carrying insects to the water.

There is one habit which the trout has which is very encouraging to the angler. It is most obvious on a river. If you catch a good-sized trout from a lie, don't imagine that's that. After you have 'rested' the water for a time, fish that lie again and you can be sure that in the 'pecking order' of trout, another one who is next in the queue will occupy it.

What kind of trout will you catch?

When you start fishing as a beginner a trout is a trout and that's that. It is only when you 'gear up' in the sport that you learn of the different kinds of trout there are in rivers and lakes.

All trout are members of the *Salmonidae* family (which includes the fish from which their name is derived — the salmon). These are:

> Brown trout *Salmo trutta*
> Seatrout *Salmo trutta*
> Rainbow trout *Salmo gairdneri*
> Cutthroat trout *Salmo clarki*
> Brook trout *Salvelinus fontinalis*
> Dolly Varden *Salvelinus malma*
> Grayling *Thymallus thymallus*

In Britain the trout you will catch will be the brown trout, the rainbow trout and occasionally the brook trout. If you like fishing in winter you may go after the grayling on rivers where this fish breeds at the opposite season to the trout.

Since rainbow trout have an irrepressible urge to go down-river to reach the sea — much to the annoyance of fish farmers who have to 'lock them up' in lakes and pools — you will fish for them in stillwaters, mostly reservoirs which are regularly stocked with their brown trout cousins. Some lakes also have brook trout stocked in them, as these fish are excellent fighters.

Of course, among the brown trout there are various strains with slightly different characteristics. Loch Leven trout from Scotland, for example, are famed all over the world for their fighting qualities. And the yellowbellies from the River Don in Aberdeenshire are also famous among anglers. Some lakes, especially in Ireland, have Gilaroo trout.

Although the seatrout is basically a brown trout which learned to migrate to the sea to get good feeding, for the angler it is something much more than that. In the first place, it is a comparatively rare fish in Britain, being found in rivers — and in a few Scottish lochs — around Ireland, Wales and Scotland. England has very few rivers supporting seatrout. Another feature exemplifying its scarcity for the angler is the fact that the seatrout migration into rivers usually only lasts a few weeks — from May till the end of July in most cases.

There is one other aspect of angling for seatrout which prohibits it being widely practised — they are best fished for at night. Indeed on some rivers this is the only feasible time to be angling for them. In Scotland, however, daytime fishing for the young, virgin seatrout is particularly popular. These are called by various names in different parts of the country — Finnock, Herling, Whitefish etc.

So far as the Cutthroat and Dolly Varden trout are concerned, you have to go to America and Canada to catch these.

In the moorland streams and hill burns which emanate from peaty soil, the usual size of trout caught is in the half-pound region, because the feeding is not so plentiful. In rivers flowing through pastoral land the trout can come out at one pound or more. In the chalk streams in the south of England three and four pounds are not unusual. Then in the stillwaters with brown and rainbow trout, the sky is almost the limit these days. Rainbow of ten to fifteen pounds have been caught.

In Scotland, seatrout caught — mainly at night — can really be any size from one to ten pounds. Indeed the record so far is over twenty pounds!

The rainbow trout

An explosion in trout fishing happened in Britain and other European countries about the turn of the century, when the rainbow trout was introduced to their waters. The main reason was the fish's remarkable growth in a relatively short period of time, and this above anything else persuaded the managements of stillwaters to introduce them for sport and for fish farms for marketing for food.

Fishing from boats is very popular. This is Queen Mother Reservoir at Datchet in Bucks.

You can tell a rainbow trout mainly by the stripe along its sides from mouth to tail, and this is either an iridescent red or various shades up to pink. It also has small black spots over its body and the tail fins are spotted. These are slightly different from the brown trout, which usually has some red spots along its middle line.

The rainbow is really a native of the western seaboard of North America, and from the north at the Bering Sea down to Southern California they are know by many different names.

They have larger appetites than brown trout and they usually move around and feed in shoals on whatever insects and fly life happens to be around at the time. It could be hatches of sedges, or march browns, or spinners. Mainly it feeds in mid-water or from the surface. It is only when there is no surface food that it will feed on the bottom on shrimp and crayfish etc.

Although many river fisheries stock their waters with rainbow, it is the stillwaters which have most of them and use them for restocking regularly, the problem about rainbow in rivers being that they tend to move downstream instinctively towards the sea, and in streams that are near the coast the fish sometimes disappear altogether. In stillwater fisheries they mix very well with brown trout.

How does the trout take the fly?

In a way, 'fly fishing' is rather a deceptive term. It would be more accurate to refer to 'insect fishing'. The impression the beginner

A plump 6lb, rainbow trout taken on wet fly.

gets about trout feeding on 'flies' is that the fish always rise to the surface to snatch the 'flies' that are alighting on the water. This is true, but only up to a point. Flies *do* fall on the surface — you can see them any time on a river or lake — but that is only a part of the story.

The cycle runs like this. The fly falls on the surface, lays its eggs, the eggs fall to the bottom, hatch out and the new-born insect struggles up to the surface as a nymph, matures rapidly, flutters its new-grown wings and if it is lucky gets away into the air to mate and produce eggs. Then the cycle begins all over again.

Now just think for a moment what you would do if you were a trout, and these insects at any stage were your main nourishment. You would first of all choose for yourself a nice secluded part of the river — say, behind a rock — where by facing upstream (and they *all* face upstream) you could see the action. You would then be able to move away from behind the rock with the minimum of effort and simply snatch the flies as they float past on the surface, or snatch them in their half-developed stage as they emerge from their eggs as nymphs. You have your food all ways.

I mention this to let you see that trout will take these insects both on and below the surface. Thus are the merits of upstream dry-fly fishing and downstream wet-fly fishing. And I expect the controversy about both these methods will continue for another hundred years. The truth of the matter is that trout will hunt for these insects at *any* stage of the flying-mating-breeding-nymphing cycle. But what about when there is no fly hatch? What would *you* do as a trout if you couldn't get your food this way?

What you must realize is that insects are both above the water and *under* the water. And there are some trout — usually the big-

Right *Many stillwater fisheries contain trout of this size — and bigger.*

Below *The dragonfly nymph is a favourite with trout.*

ger ones in lakes and reservoirs — which pay no attention to this flying-mating-nymphing cycle. They rely for their food on the thousands of insects at the bottom, some of which stay there and some of which are at various stages of getting to the surface in a slower-maturing cycle.

It was the realization of this that gave rise to those imitation insects anglers use so successfully on reservoirs and stillwaters — particularly in England — examples like The Buzzer and The Muddler. These artificial 'flies' are designed to sink and then are retrieved from the depths, and it is on this voyage that the bigger brown trout and rainbow trout snatch them. It is not unusual nowadays for these types of fly to catch trout of 9, 10 or 11 lbs. Many anglers believe that such bigger trout are better out of the water anyway, because they have become 'cannibal' and enrich their diet by devouring other smaller trout, just like pike.

Complicated? Unpredictable? Yes it is. But that is what makes trout fishing so challenging and fascinating a sport.

Chapter 4

How to start

You have bought your rod, your reel, line and cast. You have assembled them in the correct order. You are ready to fish.

Wrong. You are ready to *practise*.

Leave your waders in the cupboard — also your haversack. You will not require these for quite a while yet, because your first session will be in your own (or someone else's) back garden. What you are now about to practise is the art of casting — that is, handling the rod, line and artificial flies so that they move in harmony and eventually become like part of yourself. Skilful, smooth, effective casting is an art in itself. It deceives the trout because it lays the artificial flies as 'naturally' as possible on the water and thereby catches more fish.

Practise your casting first on dry land.

What you are now about to do is practise this casting technique with a little nut tied on to the end of your nylon leader and a tin can placed on the ground some yards further up the garden. Your aim is to stand back about six or seven paces from the can, reel out a few yards of line and try to hit the can with the nut.

The action must come from the wrist as far as the elbow — not the arm. Assuming that you are a right-handed person, take hold of the line with your left hand just above the reel. Pull off a few yards and, still holding the loose line, put your thumb on the grip handle of the rod, bring back the rod, using your wrist, so that it is over your head. Note that the rod must not be allowed to go far past the vertical on this back cast.

Then — again using a wrist motion — flick the rod forward using the pressure from your thumb to get force. The line should straighten out and the loose line in your left hand should be taken up as your little nut gathers impetus.

The nut will probably fall short of the can. This means that you need more line out. Pull off more line from the reel with your left hand and repeat the action. This time your little nut may or may not hit the can. If it over-shoots, it means you have too much line out. If it *does* hit the can you are well on the way to reasonably accurate casting.

Now, you may well ask 'If I will be fishing with three artificial flies on my cast when I am on the river, why am I practising with only one little nut on the end of my nylon?'

There are two reasons for this. The first is that one day — some might say 'the sooner the better' — you will be attracted to dry-

The comfortable grip is essential when casting a fly line.

fly fishing. This method, in my opinion difficult to learn but in the opinion of thousands of trout anglers very, very rewarding, might be considered the *real* fly fishing. Be that as it may, practising with a little nut and a tin can will certainly prepare you for that experience. In the meantime, excellence in smooth, unflurried, rhythmic casting is a 'must', whether you are fishing with three artificial flies in the downstream 'wet' style or with dry fly using one only.

The second reason is that if you become proficient at casting with only one little nut hitting a tin can, your casting on a river or a lake with any number of flies will be all the more effective. Most trout, anyway, are caught on the tail-fly, the other two flies simply adding to the deception. Therefore your flies must 'roll' out neatly.

This is a suitable stage to mention, incidentally, that there are really *four* main methods of fishing for trout with flies:

1. Dry-fly fishing upstream.
2. Artificial nymph fishing.
3. Multiple wet-fly fishing downstream.
4. Lure fishing with a sinking line and/or a weight-forward line.

Top right *Let the line adjust itself.*

Right *Learn to pause — by experience.*

Below right *Timing is essential.*

Below *When you bring the rod up the line goes overhead.*

Here are some other important points about casting:

- When you bring the rod up and your line goes overhead behind you, the purpose of this is to straighten out the line.
- Between this back cast and the forward cast you must pause briefly to let the line adjust itself. This pause varies in length of time according to the length of line you have out. Only practice tells you this.
- It is not so much the movement of the rod which causes your line to move forward properly; rather it is that pause or stopping of the rod's movements. Timing is absolutely essential in good casting and it will only be achieved by practice.
- A good, even back cast results in a good forward cast. It is like a spring releasing the 'shoot' of the line.
- Cast *backwards* hard; cast *forward* gently.
- Casting into the wind gives you a good back cast, but you will need to put more vigour from your wrist into your forward cast. The reverse is true when the wind is on your back.

Casting

It is when you start to practise casting that you realize the absolute necessity of buying matched tackle. When rod, reel and line are 'married' to each other then half the battle of accurate casting is won. If they are *not* matched, then with all the skill in the world your line will be flying all over the place, perhaps around your ears!

The most widely-used method of casting is overheard.

Unlike sea fishing or bait fishing, the weight in fly fishing is in the line itself. The line is not there simply to hold your fly as you place it in the water. The line is almost a living thing and should be an extension of the rod and your arm. For this reason, you should always be in control of the line and should not allow it to control you. The most frequent mistake made by beginners on this point is overcasting, that is bringing the rod too far back too quickly to too far forward similarly. Your casting should be conducted in a controlled, rhythmic movement between the 10 and 1 positions on a clock. Your arm should be tucked into your side and your wrist should do most of the work in a straight outward direction.

The overhead cast

The kind of casting I refer to here is the most widely-used method of overhead casting — that is bringing your flies over your head and casting them on to the surface of the water.

First, get your stance right. Stand with your feet slightly apart and make sure they are not perched precariously on unsteady rocks. *Feel* comfortable and safe.

Your grip on your rod-handle should be firm, but not vice-like. For easy balance of your rod, the position of your grip should be in the middle-to-top part of the handle. Your thumb should be on top of the handle, directed towards the top of the rod. This will give you the very necessary forward pressure, then you cast. The butt of your rod should be close to your wrist.

If you attempt to cast with too much line out, you will lose control. If too little line, your rod will not be 'loaded' properly, and again, there will be no proper control. Don't forget that the object of this exercise is to land your line, leader and flies accurately on the water *where* you wish them to go, and *how* you wish them to be presented. To do this properly, you must have a certain amount of line out, and two or three rod-lengths, gradually cast out, should do nicely. Remember your practice in your garden with the little nut and the tin can. Lift the line to the 12 o'clock position, pause as the line straightens out, then cast out.

The roll cast

There is another method of casting which is often used on a river where there is a lot of trees or foliage behind the angler, making overhead casting impossible.

Ian Bowden holding a ten-pounder and with another six trout all taken at Church Hill Farm fishery in Bucks.

It works this way. With the line in the water at your feet bring the rod tip straight up vertically. Then you 'flick' the rod-tip smartly towards the water and the line will 'roll' off the water at your feet and 'roll' out in the direction in which you flicked it. You should repeat this until the line is straight out in front of you.

If and when you graduate one day to salmon fishing, you will find the roll cast widely used, particularly on windy days when there is a strong wind at your back.

Working the fly

Depending on the current in a river, or the waves on the surface of a lake, it should be your aim to make your flies as lifelike and lively and attractive as possible to the trout. In the case of water that is not being disturbed naturally by current or wave, this means 'working' your artificial flies back to your level on the water and, at the same time, to prepare for your next cast. You do this with your non-casting hand by simply pulling the fly-line in great or small motions so that your flies move in a life-like way.

The line you are pulling should be allowed to fall at your feet (on a river) or in the boat (on a lake) and this line is allowed to 'shoot' through the rod rings at your next cast.

False casting

A false cast is just that — a cast in which the flies are maintained in the air before the next 'real' cast allows them to land on the water. Remember this about false casting — although today's fishing rods are usually made of materials which do not reflect the sun's light, it is possible that the movement of the rod could 'spook' a fish and scare it off its feeding area. Therefore the fewer false casts the better. One is usually enough.

Use the water with your casting

One of the principal aids in good casting is the water itself — or rather, how you *use* the water. A lot depends on your back cast as to how accurate and straight will be your forward cast. And the benefit of good line-lifting and back-casting is very obvious on a river where you can make use of the current.

After you have cast out your wet flies on a river, you must wait until the current takes your line downstream then, at the right time when you feel your line is properly 'loaded', you begin your back cast. Raise the rod and with your non-casting hand, gather some line as you bring the rod up to the vertical position. Then pause and cast forward, at the same time releasing the spare length of line your fingers have been holding so that it shoots through the rings.

If you do *not* wait until your line has been straightened out by the current, you will be expending needless energy in the back cast by trying to gather up unstraightened line. The cast will be rough and unpredictable and your forward cast will suffer from inaccuracy.

When you are fishing dry-fly upstream, of course, things are different. The current will not help you and you have to find by your own experience how to keep your line 'loaded' so that your back cast is properly timed.

It is the same fishing on stillwater, either from a boat or the bank. Timing is everything and plenty of practice will show you exactly when you should be lifting your line from the water to begin another cast. As with river fishing, the aim is to have your line on the water as straight as possible before back-casting.

Fishing tacklist Jim Kent demonstrates that if you have a good back cast, it is almost impossible to have a poor forward cast.

If you make a good back cast, it is almost impossible to have a poor forward cast.

Casting in a strong wind

A strong wind to an angler can be a boon or a curse, depending on where you happen to be standing. In rough days on a lake, the wind is often a great advantage in that the waves conceal the artificiality of your flies and the fish are often careless in their selection. Where the wind can be troublesome, of course, is when it is blowing against you and making casting difficult.

When you are casting into a strong wind, bring the rod down briskly on the forward cast and have the rod slightly lower than usual. 'Punch' the line out before the wind gets hold of it. On the back cast you do not require so much force.

If the wind is at your back, of course, this is all reversed as far as force is concerned. And this direction of wind can be quite a benefit in making long casts into the water.

Casting the dry-fly

If you are dry-fly fishing, much that has been said about using the water to straighten out your line etc. will be of no avail. In dry-fly fishing the general rule is 'up and across'. You fish upstream with one single fly and there is little opportunity to use the current to help in your back cast.

The main enemy of dry-fly fishing is drag. This means that your nylon leader is swept by the current so that the fly itself travels at an unnatural speed or in a different direction to the current; it is being dragged off by the leader. How do you prevent this? Some very expert anglers are plagued by it so you are not alone with the problem. Drag becomes an even worse problem when you have to cast across stream or even downstream to cover a fish you saw rising.

One obvious way of avoiding drag is simply not to cast in a direction which will cause it, even though this means ignoring some very likely water or even rising fish. But there are no hard and fast rules for the problem. The only sure answer is to use dexterity and try to keep that nylon leader up, up out of a current which will adversely affect the fly's journey. The fly *must* look and behave in a natural way.

Wading

When fishing a river you may feel that you have to get out on the water, so that you are within reasonable casting distance of where you feel the trout are lying. Don't be deluded about this, however. It may surprise you to know that there are two circumstances on a river when the fish can be almost at your feet, and wading more than a foot or so from the bank is unnecessary. The first circumstance is during a spate when the water is highly coloured; indeed just as you are concealed from the fish, so the bed of the river is concealed from you, and it is unwise to step into the unknown. In flood water trout like to keep out of the strong current, and they often lie close to the bank so that they can safely snatch any passing tit-bits of worms or other insects This means that you can either fish from the bank or, at most, a step or so into the water.

The second circumstance where wading may be unnecessary is in the evening, when darkness is falling. This is the time when the bigger fish take up their positions at the ends of pools, sometimes only a few feet from the bank from which you are fishing. Here you have to be *very* stealthy in your approach, otherwise all you will see is the shooting arrow shapes of trout taking off.

In normal circumstances, however, wading is necessary and,

like everything else in angling, there is a right way and a wrong way of doing it. I need hardly ask you to check that there are no leaks in your waders before you start, especially on your first outing of the season. Nor, I believe, do I have to remind you of the dangers of wading out of your depth and having the devastating feeling of your waders filling with water!

This latter problem, however, is more easily prevented than you might think. Most drenchings of anglers on a river are caused by one of three things — stepping into a hole, being carried off your feet by a strong current, or slipping on stones under the surface. Apart from common sense and the precaution of judging the water before you set foot in it, there is one excellent piece of equipment you can use in strange water or water which has slippery stones or deep holes or ledges to be avoided. This is a wading stick, obtained easily at fishing tacklists. If you fasten a length of string to the stick and tie it to your waist or your haversack you can release the stick to float in the water when you hook a fish, then recover it easily when the fight is over.

Wading is an activity to be practised sparingly, mainly to get away from the bank and to get clear of trees or foliage which might hamper your back cast. Never forget that once you step into the water, you are in the fish's world. This is *his* habitat and he has considerable advantages. If you stir up mud or gravel, all the fish

Left *Fishing on the River Lune. Sometimes the fish can be at your feet.*

Right *A wading stick.*

will scatter. If you step hurriedly, the trout will feel the vibrations.

On many rivers — for example on some stretches of chalk-streams in the south of England — wading is not only quite unnecessary, it is prohibited altogether.

Yes, wade if you must, but do it very carefully, as rarely as possible, and remember on a strange river that your next step forward might well be into a deep hole!

Where to go to find fishing

Anybody who really wants to fish has little difficulty these days finding out where to go. Tourist offices up and down the country have booklets, leaflets, brochures containing lists and lists of angling associations, fishing hotels and regional water boards, all offering facilities at moderate prices. And for the trout fisherman these waters are particularly accessible and most of them cheap in price, if we compare them with salmon fishing.

As a beginner, the main thing you have to remember is that you cannot fish anywhere you like without a permit. Waters — rivers and lakes — belong to somebody and if they contain fish you must have the written or printed permission of the owner before you wield a rod. These owners — or managements representing the owners — are usually local angling associations, local government authorities, private fisheries organized for the sport, or fishing hotels.

Depending on how timid or daring you feel as a beginner, there are four ways of learning to fish on a water:

- You can apply to join an angling club in your own district and go with them on their outings.
- You can take a few days' holiday at one of the fishing schools run by many hotels, whose addresses are usually listed month by month in the classified columns of the fishing magazines.
- You can take a holiday — short or long — at a fishing hotel and use its nearby river for your early steps in angling.
- You can simply walk into any fishing tackle shop, buy a permit for the local river, and fish.

Each of these methods, of course, has its benefits and disadvantages. Joining a club costs a little money in subscriptions, and

Above left *Once you step into the water you are in the fish's world.*

Left *No need to wade here. Angling photographer John Walton gets ready to net a rainbow on a reservoir.*

Above *Angling guidebooks galore.*

Below *A hotel fishing school brings you into good company.*

requires you to find a sponsoring member, but it does bring you 'into the swim' right away among fellow anglers. A hotel fishing school brings you into company with strangers, but you do get first-class tuition, and hopefully the guarantee of catching your first fish. Going to a fishing hotel can be rather daunting where you don't know anyone and find yourself among a few 'professionals' who know the local water backwards, but hotel waters are usually very good and you are assured some privacy. Conversely, taking a ticket from the fishing tackle dealer in a country village can result in you fishing with dozens of other locals, but this is usually the least expensive method.

Regardless of how you choose your fishing water, and bearing in mind that it may be your first experience at fishing, try to select a river that has a good reputation as a trout water. Some salmon and seatrout waters have virtually no brown trout in them; they support only migratory fish. Other rivers only have coarse fish and no trout. A good fishing guidebook of the district will keep you right.

Chapter 5

Fly fishing

The flies

In broad terms there are two kinds of fly for the trout fisher —
wet flies and dry flies. Put simply, the wet flies are three-on-a-
cast and they are fished across or downstream; they gradually sink
and the trout snatches one of them under the surface. The dry
fly is solo: it is fished with only one on the cast. It floats and it
is fished upstream ahead of a feeding trout so that he confuses
it with a real insect coming towards him. He snatches it, you
tighten your line and raise your rod — and, hopefully, that's that!

Another favourite wet fly—the Grouse and Claret.

Again for the sake of simplicity, and bearing in mind this piece is for the beginner in trout fishing, we will not discuss, at this stage, salmon flies, seatrout flies, artificial nymphs or buzzers or lures. Let us just concentrate on the flies you will need at the start to get you fishing for trout on a river with a reasonable chance of success.

Some artificial flies are what we term 'good old standbys' — they have proved themselves all-round catchers on most waters most of the time. For instance, I would be surprised to meet any trout angler in the country who does not carry around in his fly box a quantity of a fly called Greenwell's Glory. In my experience this fly seems to catch more trout than any other.

Other 'standbys' that seem to do very well on most waters are the Butcher, Cinnamon and Gold, Grouse and Claret, Blue and Black, Peter Ross, Invicta, and Alexandria. Indeed, if I only ever had three flies to fish with, I would choose Greenwell's Glory, the Butcher, and Grouse and Claret.

Artificial flies come in various sizes, from very tiny ones right up the scale to large ones, and they are governed by measurements which your fishing tackle dealer knows very well. Size 8 is a large one and they come down in size as the numbers go up. Size 10 is smaller, size 12 smaller still, and so on.

Small flies do well on bright spring or summer days; larger flies are needed in flood waters, and if you are fishing at sunset into the night you will need what the Scots term 'the big, black

Small flies do well on bright summer days.

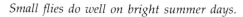

night fleas'. Another generality is that in the north of Scotland the loch trout go for larger, bushier-dressed flies, while the small, sparse ones are more successful further south.

Dry-fly fishing, in my opinion, calls for much more fastidious care in the selection of the fly. Indeed, most dry-fly anglers are obsessive about that. I don't blame them. The whole technique calls for great accuracy and cunning in everything, and I often fish with a dry-fly man who actually catches flies from above the surface of the water in a little gauze net. He than examines them carefully to see the type of fly on which the trout are feeding. When he has decided this he endeavours to match it as nearly as possible from his voluminous fly box.

The real culmination of the sport, however, is if you decide to make your own flies. The study of fly life, and the emulation of real insects on the water by fashioning them artificially, is now so much an enjoyable winter hobby for dry-fly trout anglers that it has almost taken over from the fishing itself! In most communities, fly-tying evening classes are offered at very moderate cost.

For my part — mainly because I favour downstream wet-fly fishing — I do not pay too much attention to the copying of real insects. I have a friend who ties flies for both of us and, although his inventions do not resemble real flies, they *do* catch us plenty of real trout each season.

For those who wish to enhance their interest in trout fishing by tying their own flies, the public libraries are well stocked with excellent books on the subject.

There are three main categories of fly. First there is the representative type, which are designed to look like one particular insect. Second, there are suggestive flies, which are designed in all colours to meet different conditions and different times. Thirdly there are attractor flies which, as the name suggests, simply attract the trout, although they are not necessarily replicas of real insects.

Any guidance for the beginner about which flies he should use on a particular water can never be short or concise. There is simply no hard-and-fast ruling, because conditions on a water can change hour by hour; the trout's feeding habits can change even more rapidly and — to make matters even more complex — the size and type of flies which catch trout one day will catching nothing the next.

However, here are some general observations which will be helpful for a beginner:

- Examples of 'attractor' type flies are the Kingfisher Butcher, Peter Ross and the Worm Fly.
- Fishing rough water or in a strong wind on a lake requires

Sometimes the type of fly that catches trout one day will catch nothing the next.

larger flies — say size 8. Calm, quiet water requires smaller flies and if trout are *seen* feeding, then flies as small as 16 can be used.

- If the water is cold the fly should be fished deeper and slower. It should also be larger than that used in warm water.
- Flies with a silver body such as the Butcher do well early in the season.
- If you are fishing wet-fly with three flies on the cast, consider using a winged fly on the tail, a spider pattern as the middle dropper and a Palmer on the top dropper.
- There are no undisputed 'experts' on the selection of flies for a river or a lake. Trout often take the 'wrong' fly if it is presented properly. And the reverse is the case, too. The best guidance is experience and trial and error.

Wet-fly fishing

This means what it says — fishing with two, three or even more flies on a leader downstream, which are wet because they sink gradually after you have cast them on the water. The time when the wet-fly angler has the best of it is early in the season. Under the water, his flies are often mistaken by the trout for nymphs, or even tiny fish.

Left *Trout often take the 'wrong' fly if it is presented properly.*

Right *You can smear the line with a sinking substance.*

Below *The time when the wet fly angler has the best of it is early in the season.*

What you do is this. Simply cast the flies out on the water at an angle of forty-five degrees and let them drift around in the current (assuming you are on a river). With your non-casting hand, keep a hold of a few feet of loose line so that you are ready to feel the effects of a fish which may take one of the flies. The general rule is 'a cast and a step', not only because this gives an opportunity to other anglers who may follow you down the pool, but mainly for your own sake to cover fresh water thoroughly.

If a fish takes one of your wet flies, strike him more firmly and decidedly than you might with dry-fly. Don't forget that fish face *upstream* so — unlike dry fly fishing — you are in danger of being in full view of the trout as he takes your fly. This makes too often for insecure 'takes', and many fish are lost.

Sometimes in a river the trout are not rising at all but feeding near the bottom. This is the time to change to a sinking line or one of those newer lines with a sinking tip. Alternatively, you can smear your floating line with Fuller's Earth or glycerine to make it sink. One way or another, you must get your flies right down to where the fish are. Flies near the surface — even though they are gradually sinking — are of little interest when the trout are feeding near the bottom.

Choosing the flies for wet-fly fishing

In my experience, dry-fly enthusiasts pay much more attention to the choice of flies they use than do wet-fly anglers. And the reasons are fairly evident. The dry-fliers are working with only one single fly fished upstream on the surface of the water; it *has*

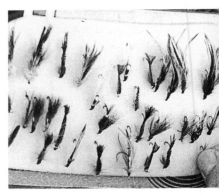

Above left *An all-round favourite fly with anglers is Greenwell's Glory.*

Above right *Some anglers say that when fishing downstream 'wet' one of the flies should always have the colour red in it.*

Below *In wet fly fishing you may not see the fish at all.*

to be the right fly, the one on which the trout are feeding, or one which may attract him to snatch.

The wet-fly angler is reasonably careful about the flies he chooses, of course, but I have met some who are fairly successful consistently and they use the same three flies on their leader each time. If I am asked to offer some very general advice on the subject of wet-fly fishing on rivers, I would say:

- Use lightly dressed flies; those big lushy things you see in tackle shops may be all right in the far north of Britain or in other countries, but otherwise — not for me.
- The spider-type flies do well in summer.
- Use a fly with red in it somewhere as an attractor, such as a Dunkeld or a Butcher, preferably on the bob.
- If in doubt, use a Greenwell's Glory, a March Brown and a Butcher as a team of flies.
- Come down in size as the season changes from spring to summer.
- Don't forget that as well as fishing wet flies downstream, you can also fish them across the current and, in warm weather, even upstream, although you have to raise the rod smartly to keep the leader from dragging.

Hooking your fish with wet flies

Unlike fishing with dry fly, the detection of a fish when it takes is tricky. In the first place, as you are fishing with your flies sinking under the surface, you may see nothing of the fish at all if it snatches one of the flies. In the second place, most of the time you will be fishing upstream of the fish. He will be facing you and if he sees you or your rod at the last moment of accepting your fly, be sure that he will get off at the speed of lightning. This means that you have to keep your eye fixed on your leader as it carries your flies down on the current. When you see that leader straightening out or behaving oddly, the chances are that you have a fish at one of your flies and you should strike at once.

When you are casting across the river, the time when a fish will often take is when your line curves in a bow. This results in the fly travelling faster, but this apparently does not dissuade the fish. On the contrary it will often dash at the fly to prevent its escape from the current.

Whether you use a floating or a sinking line, fishing wet-fly is a matter of careful judgement. For this reason, I rarely set up my tackle before I have seen the water. The place to select what

A team of wet flies.

kind of line I will use is at the river — not back at the car where I have no idea what kind of water is running. On warm summer days the trout will lie where *you* might lie if you were a fish — deep in the cool region and within easy feeding distance of a current which brings the food. In such weather, a sinking line might be best. Conversely, on cooler days, a floating line might be the thing to use.

If you are fishing in calm water on a river, don't worry too much about your flies going willy-nilly all over the place. This is how insects will be carried in such water naturally, and the trout are not put off. Sometimes if you handle the retrieval of your flies carefully, a fish will take one of them.

Some suggested wet flies

The most usual number in a team of wet flies is three — the tail or point fly, the mid-fly and the dropper. Here are some suggestions of flies to be used:

> March Brown
> Woodcock and Green
> Grouse and Claret
> Invicta

Butcher
Peter Ross
Cinnamon and Gold
Wickham's Fancy

Dry-fly fishing

The world of dry-flying is almost a holy of holies. It is the world
of the purists and the true trout fishing experts. Its adherents tend
to frown on any other means of angling for trout and, consider-
ing the traditions and history of the art, they deserve a lot of
understanding and support. This is the case not only in Britain.
In Canada, for example, I was once corrected and rebuked by a
warden on the Bow River in Calgary for wet-fly fishing — there
they call it 'streamer' fishing.

There will come a time sooner or later when you will be fishing 'dry', and I would like to warn you now that the art of upstream
dry-flying is a difficult one to acquire and takes a lot of practice.
Yet — and I must say this, too — it is the most rewarding, inspir-
ing method I know for catching trout. On many of the chalk-
streams in the south and west of England any other method is
unthinkable, and even forbidden.

Some people who are reading this might even suggest that
it is where I should have begun, that the dry-fly is the *only* real
method of fly fishing, and indeed it is more productive, and certainly more challenging. They may be right. Anyone who sets out
to teach others how to do anything must begin and continue on
the basis of his own experiences and I must say that I had to
progress towards dry-fly fishing from 'downstream wet'.

As briefly and as clearly as I can, I would like to explain what
happens.

First, you must remember that fish face upstream when feeding. This means that if you are standing behind them, either in
the water or on the bank, they cannot see you. And if you remain
stock-still, like a heron, the chances are they cannot feel or hear
you either. This gives you a tremendous advantage.

Next, what you require to do if you want to catch a trout which
you can see feeding (or at least see the signs of it) is place one
single fly upstream of it, let it float down and the trout mistakes
it for a real insect and snatches it.

Sounds simple? Believe me, it is not. And here is why:

● The trout must be a *surface*-feeding fish. If it is not, your floating fly will not reach him.

Left *Expert John Roberts recommends these dry flies — Iron Blue Dun, All Black Fly, Parachute Greenwells and Houghton Ruby.*

Right *Rises are not always easy to spot.*

- The artificial fly you choose for the job must imitate the actual kind of fly on which the trout is feeding at that time. The selection therefore is critical.
- The nylon leader you use must be tapered, either as one complete cast or made up very carefully in graduated stages of three or four lengths.
- Your casting must be very accurate, straight and unflurried. Sometimes this entails long casting if you have to stand many yards downstream of the fish, either on the water or on the bank.
- Your fly must float, and after so many casts it must be 'treated' with a floatant substance to keep it in that condition. This flotation material comes as a little aerosol spray and can be bought in the tackle shop.
- You must endeavour after casting to keep your nylon leader free of the water, so that it does not drag the fly at an unnatural pace. Otherwise the trout will see at once that it is not a real fly. This means that you have to use great dexterity immediately your fly lands on the water.

The difficulties could go on and on. But so can the benefits. Many dry-fly anglers I know tell me that this is not only the *true* method of fly fishing, it is also the most successful.

I cannot vouch for that statement. All I do know from my own dry-fly trips is that when I catch a trout there is no thrill quite like it. And if you have the added bonus of having caught a trout this way using a fly you yourself have made, the reward is twofold.

Fishing in the rough water

As spring becomes summer and the days grow warmer, trout move into the more turbulent water of the streams or a river — or rather, they take up their territorial rights just off the more disturbed water or behind rocks. This is where they will lie so that with the least amount of energy all they have to do is move out and snatch insects as they are carried by the current. Another reason why they favour lies like this in the rough water is that it is well oxygenated and cool in the warm summer days.

By day, this is where you should be if you are fishing dry-fly. Take up your stance quietly so that you can cast upstream and slightly across the current. Use your eyes. Look into the disturbed water for the slightest sign of a rising fish. Yes, they are there all right — look...look.

Then, when you think you see signs of a trout in that white water, get ready to cast above him. Peel off some line, take a couple of false casts then let your fly settle gently about a foot above where you saw the rise. Rises are not easy to spot at first but constant practice will teach you to see them.

You have to be very attentive to catch fish this way. If you do not strike at all as a result of missing seeing the fish going for your fly, you will lose him, of course. On the other hand if you strike too quickly you will also lose him by taking the hook from his mouth. The real skill — and most good dry-fly anglers develop it — is in knowing just when to strike. And by 'strike' I really mean 'tighten' in a steady, firm but gentle movement of raising the rod

Left *A spray can of floatant for dry flies.*

Below *A small piece of chamois leather for drying out the fly.*

and taking spare line up with your non-casting hand.
If you do catch a fish, wade quietly to the bank and despatch it as quickly and humanely as possible. Don't be in a hurry to resume fishing. Take your time. It should be obvious to you that the dry fly you chose was a fair replica of what the trout was going for naturally. That should give you some satisfaction about your judgement. And you would be wise to fish with the same fly again.
Reel in. Examine your fly carefully. Is it clean and in good order. If not, give it a swirl in the water. Then dry it off carefully with the little square of chamois leather which you keep for that purpose. Put the fly in the fold of the chamois and press — that is all that is necessary. Then apply more floatant and see that the hackles or wings of the fly are standing up and looking natural. You are ready to start again.

Fishing in the pools

While you have been fishing in rough water you are almost bound to have seen the rings of rising fish in the pools above and below the stream. During the day in summer ignore them. They are not at all easy to catch in clear water.
It's when the first shades of dusk gather — that is the time to fish these pools. And as the light fades, so your chances of catching fish here improve and improve, until the fishing is at its very best by nightfall.
Don't be misled into thinking that these tell-tale rings on the surface are made by small fish. Some of the biggest trout in the river make the smallest signs.
Take up your stance at the end of the pool, slightly to one side so that any darkness offered by a high banking or by trees helps to conceal you. Peel off some line quietly and cast your fly into the gently flowing water, then retrieve it just as it reaches the beginning of the rough stream.

Fishing into the evening

There is no doubt that fishing the evening rise well into the deep dusk with dry fly is one of angling's finest experiences.
You fish the pools because as the sun goes down in summer the trout move from the streams into the quiet pools, and there they take up their residence at the ends of the pools. While you

will stand a good chance of catching fish with the same fly as you used in the streams, my preference is to put on a slightly larger fly and a slightly heavier cast — say with a tapering coming down at the point to 3 or 4 lb breaking strain.

Of course you came prepared for the evening rise, didn't you? This is why you are carrying at least two spare casts in your pocket or haversack, because if you get into a tangle you don't want to be spending valuable time trying to sort it out. Take it off and replace it at once. And, of course, you brought a torch with you, didn't you? And you *do* know your way back to your car, because by the time the best of the fishing ends it will be quite dark.

Once you have taken up your stance at the end of the pool, do not wade unless it is absolutely essential. You will soon see why if you take even one step. The ripple and rings on the water from your movement will spread right over the whole surface of the pool and possibly spook all the fish for a time.

If you *do* wade and cause such a disturbance, you will have to wait five minutes or so for the ripples to settle down. And five minutes at this 'bonanza' time on a river is a lot of valuable fishing gone.

Fishing before dawn

There is an old angling saying, 'In summer you can't have your sleep *and* your fish as well.'

There is a lot of truth there, particularly if you want to be on the river when the most fish and the biggest fish are most vulnerable to your fly. Apart from the evening rise, the other period of greatest opportunity is just before dawn, when the first grey light appears in the east. This is the time to be on the river in the same position and with the same stance that you took up in the evening.

There is about an hour at this time of the day when the fly fishing is superb. You get to the river in the darkness, you wait till the first glow of dawn shows, and you start fishing.

Fishing in a strong wind on the river

When the weather is brisk and there is a strong wind, the place to be on a river with your dry fly is in the pools. The wind will make little difference to the rough water, but what a difference it makes to the otherwise smooth surface of a pool! Then it looks like a little lake with the ripples and waves going over the surface. These are excellent for concealing your movements and for confusing the fish.

You can afford to impart little twitching movements to the fly as you cast upstream. The slow current will still carry your fly downstream towards you, of course, but with the same dexterity as you used in the rough water you should be able to keep that nylon leader from dragging.

Good fish can be caught more easily in a pool of a river on a blustery, choppy day than otherwise.

Flashing leader

The nylon leader you use, particularly on a bright day, occasionally flashes and this can put a trout off at the very moment he is tempted to take your fly. You can buy a substance — Fuller's Earth, for instance — which will take away this flash. Or you can simply use some soil from the near bank.

John Roberts dry fly fishing the River Dove in Yorkshire.

The leader shows

It is essential that the last few inches of your nylon leader should not float with the fly. If it does, the trout will see instantly the shadow and that something is not natural, even though your artificial fly is an exact replica of what he is seeking. The answer to this problem is the same as the one above — smear some earth on the leader.

Fish are rising but will accept no dry fly

You must not imagine that tell-tale rings on the surface necessarily indicate fish rising for flies. They may be nymphing — getting the insects in the pupae stage as they rise from the bottom. If so, it is time for you to change to artificial nymph.

Fish are rising for flies but you cannot see what sort of flies

Now you are in for a guessing game. If you are sure there are flies and the fish are certainly feeding on them, try a succession of tried-and-true patterns like Tup's Indispensable, or the Black Gnat or the Grey Duster.

These little double-hooked flies are favourites in Loch Leven in Scotland.

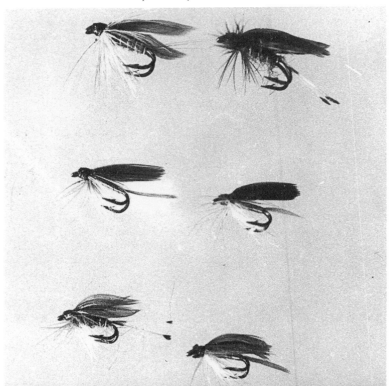

The nylon leader keeps dragging
Drag is the dry-fly anglers' worst enemy — when the line and/or the leader are on the water travelling at a different speed to that of the fly. On seeing the effect of this on the fly the trout knows at once that something is wrong, and he won't touch the fly.

When you are sure that you are casting correctly and still experiencing drag, take up a different position on the river so that you and your line and leader stand a better chance of depositing the fly without drag. Don't persist in an impossible position.

The fish are taking the fly but escaping almost at once
It is possible you are striking too fast and pulling the fly out of the trout's mouth before he can take a proper hold. Don't forget your lesson on this thing sometimes mistakenly called 'striking'. Keep your head, be calm, raise your rod, tighten the line steadily and keep the rod up till you are sure the fish is hooked properly.

The wind is blowing downstream
A downstream wind is a nuisance to the dry-fly angler. But when you experience this handicap, don't despair. What is a downstream wind at one part of a river may well be a cross wind at another, particularly if the river winds to and fro in its travel.

There is nothing very bad about a cross-stream wind for the dry-fly fisher. Indeed such a wind on the surface of the water can help to conceal him and his leader from the fish.

Some generalities about the flies to use

The number, size, pattern, shape and colours of artificial flies are almost endless in variety. As a beginner you will be quite understandably bewildered. What flies to use? What size? Single or double-hooked? Hackled or not? What pattern? Any author writing about fishing can only give general advice based on his own experiences. And I am no different.

Naturally you will have made up your mind whether you want to fish upstream 'dry' or downstream 'wet'. That's basic. 'Dry' flies are just that; they float on the surface of the water and in nearly every case they must be accurately imitative of the real thing on which the fish are feeding at that time. 'Wet' flies? Well, the scope is a little broader, mainly because you are offering three flies downstream to the waiting fish and it has always been my experience that for some reason the trout are not quite so fastidious about the pattern or colour, with certain obvious limitations. (For example, there are some rivers where only a green-coloured wet fly is acceptable, others where only a fly with some blue in it is acceptable.) It has been said by some fishing experts that an angler fishing downstream wet should *always* have a fly with the colour red in it. That is a matter for experience.

Without knowing where you plan to fish, or when you intend fishing, at what time of the year, time of day, in what kind of weather and in what level of water, let me offer ten simple items of generalized advice about flies:

- If possible, buy your artificial flies from the tackle dealer near the water; he is a local man and he knows what the trout will accept at any time of the year.
- Small flies with double hooks are very good on some lakes, because they sink well and imitate surface-seeking insects.
- Greenwell's Glory is the most favoured trout fly among anglers. Some say no cast should be without one, and I would agree.
- Smaller flies are best by day, especially if it is bright, and in low water. As evening approaches, the larger flies do best. At night it is usually time to use the really large, blackish

A John Veniard selection of Matuka lures for stillwaters — three on the left down are: Olive Matuka, Parson's Glory. Badger and Red. Three on the right down are; Grey Matuka, Kent's Gold, Kent's Silver.

'night' flies, the tail-fly with a flash of silver on it, like a Butcher.

- In flood water, if the trout are taking flies at all, you can comfortably afford to 'move up' in size so that the fish can see what you are offering.
- On most Scottish Highland lochs the trout go for larger, bushy flies.
- On English stillwaters containing larger rainbow and brown trout, fish deep with slightly heavier flies like the Muddler or the Buzzer.
- Don't throw away tatty old flies that look 'past their best'. On some rivers like the Clyde, it is precisely these dingy old, sparse-haired flies the trout snatch.
- When fastening wet flies to your cast make sure that they are all of the same size. Fish notice odd-size 'eccentricities' and avoid them; they don't seem natural.
- Watch the flies the locals use. They know.

Chapter 6

On a river

Some advantages of fishing a river

Trout live in rivers, lakes and estuaries. Generally speaking, brown trout are in the rivers and lakes, rainbow trout are in the lakes, and those trout that are inhabitants of the estuaries — as distinct from migratory seatrout — are pink-fleshed, called by various names like Slob Trout.

If you are wondering whether you should start your hobby of angling on a river or on a stillwater (assuming that you have a choice), consider some of the advantages of river fishing.

I believe, and I hope you would agree with me, that it is the fishing, not the fish, which is important about this sport. In other words, I would like to think that you have decided to take up trout fishing as much for its environment and its surroundings as for the fish you may catch. If that is so, I believe you will enjoy yourself more along the banks of some lovely river than on some barren, featureless sheet of water like a reservoir or a bleak hill loch.

Don't mistake me. Not for the world am I making judgements about the psychological rewards you may get or miss from either kind of water. What I am suggesting is that at the beginning of your trout-fishing career you may find better enjoyment (although perhaps smaller fish) on a river than on a lake. But if it is big trout you really want, then by all means head for one of those many new trout reservoirs and stillwaters which have them, scenery or not.

There is another thing about trout fishing which will appeal to you — the variety of water-flow. A river gives you the opportunity to practise 'reading' the water, assessing your own skill in judging where the trout may be feeding. And every step of the way along a river bank, every turn, every bend brings a new vista,

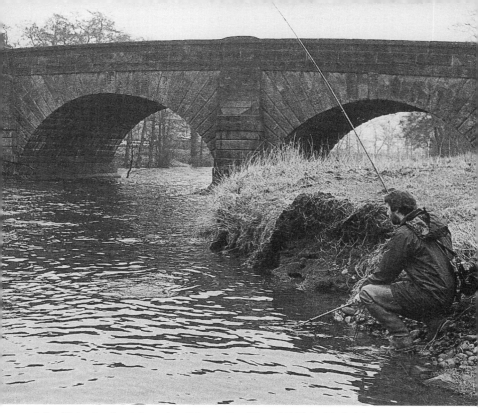

John Roberts about to net a fish on the River Nidd in Yorkshire.

a new stretch of unexplored water and a new challenge. Further, by dextrously casting your flies at the right spot, you stand an excellent chance of hooking a fish.

The more laborious and tedious cast-after-cast routine on a stillwater, *can* become boring, even though there is the chance of a big fish taking your fly.

Personally I have always found another great benefit about fishing a river — my wife and family enjoy the outing if the weather is fine. Rivers do not separate man and wife in fishing quite so much as sea-angling or stillwater fishing.

This is not to say that family picnics and fishing outings always go hand-in-hand. What I *am* saying is that they are not at all incompatible pursuits.

One other thing about rivers. Most fishing hotels own or control stretches of river, rather than lakes or stillwaters. And to the guests at these hotels 'the river' is the centre of attention, angling skill, discussion and good catches. If you go for a holiday to a fishing hotel it is usually the river that will be the focus of *your* attention.

Where to find the trout on a river

As a beginner you would be forgiven for thinking that the trout are everywhere and anywhere on a river. Not so. As I advised you in the piece about how trout feed, you must stalk your fish — use your eyes, look for the places where *you* might lie if you were a fish, look for any signs of a feeding trout such as the telltale rings, and remember that in the moving water of a river the place where the ring starts is where the trout will be, not where the ring travels.

In my own experience, the places where I like to fish for trout are threefold. Here they are:

In the rough water

In the bright, warm days of summer, many trout like to enjoy the cool, well-oxygenated water in the rougher parts of a river. They will often lie behind rocks so that all they have to do to feed is move over very slightly to catch the occasional fly or other insect as it comes downstream. In this situation trout are often difficult to catch by the wet-fly method, but a dry-fly fished with dexterity upstream can be very profitable. I have seen many trout over a period taken this way by a dry-fly expert who knew how to remain stock-still *behind* the feeding trout, how to make the minimum of disturbance and how to select exactly the right fly to attract the fish.

Where the rough water fans out into a current

Again, this sort of spot can be excellent in summer, particularly in the early morning or late evening. This is where many trout lie in relaxation, feeding on the insects coming down.

Wet-fly fishing is the best approach here, in my opinion, and the first few casts are usually the most profitable. After that, no matter how carefully you wade, the fish will probably 'go off'. Perhaps they become wary by the mere suspicion of an angler being there.

As evening light fades, however, there is less chance of the trout being 'spooked' and if you make as little movement as possible — perhaps lengthening your line slightly at every cast — you may catch quite a few fish in an hour.

Right at the end of pools before the next rough water starts

Fishing either wet-fly or dry-fly, this is my favourite spot on a trout river, and in my experience is the ideal casting area for the big fellows in the darkening of a summer evening. Indeed, so bold are those trout as darkness is falling, that it is quite possible to hear them as they feed and, if the light is still there, to see the widening rings sometimes only a few yards from where you are standing.

As it gets darker, of course, dry-fly fishing upstream from the edge of the rough water into the smoother water becomes more difficult. And in the darkness itself you will find that wet-fly fishing from a suitable stance can bring some large fish.

Your flies should be larger in the deepening dusk, and at night as big as size 10s.

'Read' the river

There you are, wearing your waders and your haversack, standing on a river-bank and looking across the water as you hold your line and, of course, you have hooked the tail-fly on to the little ring just above the cork handle of your rod. Or at least you have hooked it on to the first ring of your rod, to keep the cast in place and prevent the flies from blowing around and perhaps hooking somebody's ear — hopefully not your own. What do you do?

There is no sense in fishing 'barren' water. Trout in their feeding habits are generally predictable; they like certain 'lies', and usually these are the places where they can leisurely drift out, snatch a passing insect as it floats downstream, then drift back again behind the shelter of a rock or some weeds. Minimum effort, maximum feeding, very natural and efficient.

These are the spots to look for. And mostly you will find them at the ends of the runs — say, where the rough, white water is beginning to smooth out and glides and spreads on its way downstream. Watch those areas carefully, and if you are lucky and if it is 'feeding time', it is there that you may see the occasional telltale ring or circle of a trout feeding. Beware, however — these rings drift downstream with the current. The place where the trout is feeding is exactly where and when the circle on the water starts. At that instant the fish has just sucked in an insect. What you have to do is offer your cast of three flies so that he is deceived, and hooked.

You have a choice. You are fishing 'wet' fly and that means that your three flies must be placed on the water above where the trout is feeding, so that they drift downstream, sinking gently and gradually. Therefore the first option you have is to wade quietly upstream a good bit away from the trout altogether, cast your flies into the rough water and let them be carried by the current down to the trout. The advantage? The rough water will conceal you and your rod and line from the trout and he may snatch one of your flies — usually the tail one — in the belief that it is a real sinking insect. The disadvantage is that if the rough water does not conceal you — and don't forget fish always face upstream — he will not be fooled, and will ignore your flies.

The other choice you have is to move downstream below the trout and cast your flies above him into the rough water. The advantage? The trout cannot see you as he is facing upstream. The disadvantage is that upstream wet-fly fishing is, in my opinion, very difficult, because somehow you have to keep your nylon cast clear of the water and prevent it looping or moving downstream ahead of your flies.

You have another choice, a compromise. You can cast your flies *across* the current, and perhaps get the benefit of both advantages. It may work.

Making these decisions is the part of trout fishing that requires judgement, strategy and timing. Your decision depends on so many things — the strength of the flow of the water, the light on the water, your position, the trout's position, and most of all your experience and confidence in presenting your flies deceptively.

My recommendations? Well, going by my own experience as a beginner, I would position myself well upstream of the fish — perhaps above the rough water altogether — and I would peel off plenty of line. Then I would cast my flies into the rough water, let them drift down easily and gently so that my tail-fly reached the trout at the right depth. Then — ?

That's all the fun of fishing.

NOW *you are ready to start*

At long last you are at the waterside. Let's say it is a river. *Don't* wade into the water. *Don't* cast your flies yet. *Don't* make any disturbance near the water. Stand well back from the edge of the river and *study* it. Then ask yourself these questions:

- How deep is the water? Does the depth change? Where does it change?
- How fast or slow is the water moving? Does it move at the same rate right along the stretch I am observing?
- How is the bottom? Is it likely to be rocky, or gravelly, or muddy, or what?
- If *I* were a trout, and knowing what I have been taught about its feeding habits, where would I be in this stretch of the river?

Above *Cast flies into the rough water and let them drift down easily.*

Below *Study the water before you cast a line.*

- Does it appear that there could be hazards on this stretch of river (such as precipitous shelving out from the bank)?
- Do I know just where I will make the first few casts of my flies on the water?
- Can I imagine what the fish will see?
- Am I remembering to tread lightly and avoid unnecessary vibration from my footsteps on the bank?
- Am I remembering that some trout might well be lying close to the bank from which I am fishing?
- How can I avoid my shadow falling on the water if there is bright sunshine. Am I in the right part?

Now you may approach the water — *quietly*.

You are wearing your waders. This does not mean that you *must* wade. Waders are to enable you to cast over a fish which you could not reach from the bank. They also enable you to stay low, out of the skyline, and lessen your visibility. It is better for you to start fishing from dry land or, at the most, ankle-deep in water. Be prepared when you make your first cast. In my experience, a feeding trout very often accepts the first offer of an artificial fly from an angler, and you should be ready to strike when the fish takes your fly.

Let me explain hastily what the word 'strike' means. In a way it is a misnomer. When a trout takes your fly you will instantly feel the 'take'. Your leader and line will straighten, the point of your rod will bend and this is when you perform the action called 'striking'. All you do is raise your rod to tighten the line and leader against the fish, and by doing so you set the hook in its mouth. Do all this in a steady, firm, unhurried motion and the fish is not likely to get off. 'The one that got away' is usually caused by too hurried to too slow striking. I explain this striking business right away at this stage in case your first cast hooks your first fish and you are not sure what to do.

Now let me explain how you get the fish to the bank, despatch it and take it in your bass bag proudly home to your family.

The trout is hooked. You are holding your rod up and keeping strain on him to prevent him either tearing the hook from his mouth or otherwise getting free. Your immediate considerations should be — how heavy is the fish? Half-a-pound? Two pounds? Heavier? What is the breaking strain of the nylon leader you are using? How cautious must you be in playing him? If he is a heavy fish and you are using a light leader should you give him more line to let him run then carefully ease him in as he tires? Or can you safely get him in quite smartly?

Now you use your net. Bring the fish over the net and scoop

Above *How heavy is the fish? What is the breaking strain of the leader?*

Below *A spit of land is an ideal spot on a stillwater for fishing.*

him into it with one firm, unhurried motion. Go to the bank. Don't attempt to dislodge the fly from his mouth out in the river. Get well away from the water so that if he does break free he will not land in the river again where you have no hope of recovering him. Administer the 'last rites' with your priest instantly and humanely. Then dislodge the fly from his mouth and put the fish in your bass. Don't leave the dead fish on the river bank, otherwise a greedy gull may spot it and make a meal of it.

So much for catching — unexpectantly — your first fish.

How to hook your fish

Attracting the trout to your flies is only the start. Next he has to take one of them. Then *you* have to make sure he is well hooked, by striking, making sure that the hook is securely imbedded.

How do you do this? Well, it is a lot simpler than you might imagine, providing you keep your head, don't get excited and do everything in a controlled, gentle rhythm. When you feel (or sometimes see) your fish taking your fly, it means he has it in his mouth. A trout's reaction is tremendously fast — much faster than yours or mine. Therefore, as soon as he feels the faintest prick of the hook he can spit out your fly and that's that. You've lost your fish.

You can lose a fish in any one of a dozen ways. Perhaps you have too much line out and the 'telegraph' message takes too long to reach you from the fly and up your rod. Perhaps your length of line is quite appropriate but your nylon cast itself is slack as it drifts into quieter water. Perhaps you are too slow on the uptake and too late in getting the message.

Let's assume that you *do* feel or see your fish taking your fly. If you strike in the normal meaning of that word, either by jerking your line with your left hand or jerking your rod, you have little chance of catching the fish. Trout are very fast in getting out of danger, and you will be left with that sickening, saddening limp line that signals another fish lost. Simply raise your rod smoothly and steadily, and keep hold of your line in your non-casting hand. Then you will know two essential things — whether you *have* hooked the fish, and whether it is a big one or not. If it is a small fish there is no problem. You can likely bring him to your net in one steady sweep. If he is a big fish, however, say a trout of a pound or over, you may have a battle on your hands.

Holding and netting one of these larger trout brings out the real angler, because he has to consider so many things all at once: the breaking strain of his nylon cast, whether the hook is properly embedded, his own wading position, his net, whether the fish

Is the fish ready for the net?

will run downstream or not, or if he runs upstream, how he can maintain a proper tension to keep the trout firmly hooked. And most particularly he has to consider exactly when the fish tires and is ready to be netted. The best place in the trout's mouth for a successful hooking and landing is in the 'scissors' of the jaw, at the hinge.

In this connection, trout fishing is not very different from salmon fishing — just smaller in scale.

You've hooked your fish — now what?

A trout has shown an interest in your fly. You have seen him rise, but for some reason he will not take the fly in his mouth. What do you do?

Cast over him again, at the same place and in the same way. It is far better to have a go again and again at a fish which you *know* is there, than to fish blindly elsewhere on the water for fish which may or may not be in the vicinity. If the fish still ignores your fly, change the fly. You may strike it lucky with a different pattern or size.

- If you are fishing wet-fly downstream, strike as quickly as possible when you feel the pull of a taking fish.
- If you are nymphing, strike when the fish is seen to take the fly.
- When dry-fly fishing, wait till the fish takes the fly below the surface, then strike.

Playing the fish

If you are fishing a river and wading, make for the shore as soon as possible. Yes, there *are* some expert anglers who prefer to remain

Don't sweep the net under the fish.

in the current of a good, wide part of the river and catch and kill their trout out there, putting them one at a time into a bag or a creel slung over their shoulders. I have seen them. But that method is not for me, nor do I recommend it for you.

Keep a steady contact with the fish as you wade carefully ashore. Keep the rod bent in tune with the fish's movements, and keep the line straight. Keep strain on the fish, and that way he will not get off. Compensate for the jerks and pulls of the fish, allowing it to run when necessary, then retrieving line when you can. And remember to keep that rod held high.

The fish will tire eventually, until it starts to turn on its side. That's your sign that he is possibly ready for the net. Be ready, however, for a last-minute lunge. Look for a place to land the fish, and take it steadily and firmly to that spot — preferably in the slack water, out of the current.

Dip your landing net into the water so that it is completely submerged. Then draw your fish over it and raise the net at once. *Don't* sweep the net under the fish.

What do you do with the fish?

You have your fish safely in the net. You walk with it right up on the bank. What now?

If you wish to kill the fish to take it home, do this quickly and humanely with your priest. Two or three sharp knocks on the head above the eyes should do it. You should do all this before trying to remove the fly from its mouth.

But perhaps you do *not* wish to kill the fish, but return it to the water. (Note that all undersized fish *must* be returned to the water. Your permit will tell you what is meant by 'undersize'.) You have to do this with great care. Keep the fish away from sand and grit, as its skin and scales are very vulnerable to abrasion. Your hands must always be wet when handling.

Don't throw the fish into the water; the shock may kill it. Slide the fish gently with your wet hand into the water and if it remains stationary help it along by moving it gently forward. (Pulling it backwards will drown the fish.) If this fails, kill the fish at once.

A word about netting

In the fishing tackle shop, you will see all shapes and sizes of nets. One of the most popular I have seen, especially in North America, is a small thing about the size of a tennis racket. It looks and feels wonderful, and carrying it is easy. In my opinion, I wouldn't have one at any price.

You have to think about many things before you buy or carry a net to the water: portability, size of fish you might expect, ease of handling on the water. In my estimation, better be sure than sorry, and for this reason I prefer a long-handled net with a good diameter. No nonsense.

The way to net a trout successfully after he has been hooked is this: First make sure he is ready for the net — either that he has tired and given up the struggle or that the quicker he is in the net the better, since the hook-hold does not seem too secure.

No fish is caught until he is safely in the net, and this means that your netting operation has to be done with as much stealth and skill as your fishing. Do nothing hurried or noisy. Move your net under the water and let it remain there while you draw the fish over it. Then lift the net in a steady, deliberate sweep upwards to engulf the fish. Hold it up and wade to the shore. If you intend to keep it, deliver the *coup de grâce* instantly, before extracting the hook. If not, wet your hands and extract the hook carefully, before holding the fish facing upstream and gently releasing it.

Fishing from a boat, an adequate landing net is essential. That means one with a long handle, so that you are not scrabbling about against the boat trying to net a big fish with a short-handled net.

Chapter 7

On a stillwater

Where to find the trout on a lake or reservoir

There are two ways of fishing a lake: from the bank, or from a boat. The advantages of fishing from a boat are obvious — you can cover more water, and a skilled oarsman can 'drift' the boat to where there are trout feeding. However, bank fishing is very popular among regular anglers on certain stillwaters. The hire of a boat can be quite expensive, and fishing from the bank *can* produce good results when fish move in to shallow water.

Bank fishing

Trout often lie or feed in certain areas on a lake. In reservoirs you can often strike lucky near dam walls or towers. Other 'hot' areas are in bays, or where the bed is shallow. Around weed beds is a good area because of the insect life generated there, and for the same reason where trees overhang the bank.

As if in contradiction of these guidelines, good trout are often found at promentaries, in rocky areas and where fences or walls enter the water (you often find these in a recently built reservoir which has flooded over what was farmland).

My favourite area for angling, however, is one that rarely lets me down, and that is at the mouth of an inflowing river or stream. The reason seems to me obvious — that is where the fish will be lying to catch the insect life coming down the lake.

The difficulty for a novice fishing from the bank of the lake is finding out for himself where he should be casting his flies. Well-known 'hot spots' are often overcrowded with anglers. And even the advice he gets from the locals may be contradictory or

In reservoirs you can often be lucky at the dam wall.

(dare I say it?) deliberately misleading.

My advice is to rely on your own good sense. And keep asking yourself the sensible questions — where would *you* be on the lake if you wanted to get the maximum food for the minimum effort, with the best chances of concealment?

Look for the signs of rising fish, the tell-tale rings. Observe the direction of the wind, and the angle of the sun. Don't be in a hurry. Approach the water gently and do not wade at first. Look behind to see what foliage or trees might interfere with your casting. Increase your casting distance gradually, then wade in the water cautiously as a last resort.

Keep your flies moving on the water, either by short little jerks or long, slow pulls. Experiment. And at all times try to keep your line fairly tight so that if and when a fish takes, you have a reasonable chance of striking and setting the hook properly.

Boat fishing

The usual arrangement on a boat is for three anglers, two fishing at any time from either end of the boat and one on the oars guiding the boat and keeping it in a steady drift. Then they change round at regular intervals.

On some lakes, particularly reservoirs, no tailboard motors are permitted, although non-polluting electric motors may be allowed. On others, such as Loch Leven in Scotland, an outboard motor is the only feasible way of getting the boat to the best fishing spots on such a vast water.

The only additional item of tackle you may need for fishing from a boat is a drogue, which is simply a sheet of canvas with ropes and used as a sort of underwater parachute. It is slung over the side of the boat to slow it during its drift. Without a drogue, in a stiff breeze, the boat may well travel far too quickly and reach the leeward bank before any decent fishing can be had. Moreover, with a drogue fixed to the bow the angler may fish across the wind on either side of the boat.

There *is* an alternative to a drogue, of course, and that is simply an anchor. Another method is for the oarsman to work into and across the wind, each person in turn taking his share of the rowing.

As the boat is drifting into 'fresh' water, and in theory towards the fish, it is rarely necessary to cast very far. And it is sensible to draw the flies towards the boat in the retrieve in a steady motion as a fish may well be following them. Depending on the conditions and the frequency of fish rising, either a floating or sinking line can be used. My motto is, 'If what I am doing is not catching fish — change.' I change flies, change lines and even change methods frequently.

Nymph fishing

This is another aspect of wet-fly fishing. Never forget that the trout takes 90 per cent of its food *under* the water. This is why wet-fly fishing on a lake is usually much more effective than fishing with dry fly on the surface. So it is sensible to assume that when no feeding fish are showing any signs at all on the surface, it is in fact time to get underneath to where the fish *are* feeding.

This question of depth is all-important. On certain days and under certain conditions the trout will be at a certain level. There is hardly any way to tell day by day where this level may be. Trial and error is the only answer.

Over varying periods of time, various insects like midges and sedges change into nymphs and pupae, which eventually rise and hatch into the adult flying insect. Trout feed on these insects at every stage, and if you wish to fish with an artificial nymph you should make them move in a series of slow jerks by retrieving them to the surface. There are various kinds of nymph flies on

Casting a nymph on a natural lake in early spring.

sale in the tacklist's shop, of course, but here are three I would recommend:

Tail-fly	:	Pheasant tail nymph	Size 16–12
Mid-fly	:	Green or brown nymph	Size 14–10
Dropper	:	Invicta	Size 14–10

Lure fishing

It was really the explosive growth of the cultivation of rainbow trout and their introduction into lakes and reservoirs which brought about the parallel growth in lure fishing — that is fishing with a large, feather-constructed thing which is more like an underwater creature than a fly. Certainly lures have been used for many years in fishing for seatrout and, yes, brown trout as well. But it is the rainbow which is the most popular quarry with lures such as the Buzzer or the Ace of Spades or the Muddler.

Bank fishers on many reservoirs go in for 'long-lining' with weight-forward lines or shooting heads. They make many long, false casts before letting the lure alight on the water. Then they retrieve the line by hand in small jerks. And without doubt the method is highly successful in catching big fish — some as heavy as 10 lb.

The method is very suitable on stillwaters, but it is rarely used on a river.

Dry-fly fishing on a lake

This is usually a second choice method of fly fishing in stillwaters. There are two main ways of using the dry fly:

- One single fly, carefully selected to match what the trout is feeding on, is treated with a floatant, usually a silicone substance. You allow the fly to rest on the surface of the water, then you twitch the line at intervals to attract the fish.
- The second way is to use two dry flies on a prepared leader

Lead-headed lures called Dog Nobblers are best fished on a floating line in deep water with a 'sink and draw' action.

— one on the tail, and the other as a dropper. The tail-fly is usually a nymph pattern. When a trout takes the dry fly, it often does so savagely, so you must be ready for a 'smash hit'.

Dapping

Although I do not necessarily recommend the purchase of the equipment needed for this interesting method of fishing on a lake, it *is* the most appropriate spot to describe what has often been called 'the duffer's fishing method' simply because luck plays a bigger part in its success than skill. It is also very thrilling when a fish is caught. Here is how it works.

The first thing you need is a dapping rod of 12–14 feet. I *have* used a long salmon rod for dapping, but quite frankly the collapsible, telescopic dapping rod made for the job is better.

The next thing you need is a length of dapping floss. This is a woolly-looking line made of tiny strands of silk floss. A rod's length of this is tied to your ordinary nylon leader, then another short leader of 4 feet is tied to this. You fasten your dapping fly on to this second leader and you are ready. One other thing you need is a good, stiff breeze.

Dapping flies are big bushy things to which is applied a floatant, either in ointment form or from an aerosol spray. One com-

Dapping for trout on a Scottish loch. Note the long dapping rods.

monly used fly in Scottish lochs is the Loch Ordy.

You hold the dapping rod upright in the boat. No casting, as such, is necessary. All you have to do is allow the breeze to carry the silk floss — and your fly — right out over the water. Then you let it 'kiss' the surface and raise it slightly so that it 'daps' like this from spot to spot, preferably just touching each little wave as it dances.

You will be in no doubt when a fish takes the fly. The effect is electric. The fly will disappear under the surface, your silk floss and line will straighten out and there you have your fish. The rest — bringing him to the net — is up to your skill.

One thing about dapping worth mentioning is that for some reason the method often attracts bigger fish. In fact on some Scottish seatrout lochs like Loch Maree and Loch Sheil, they catch fish over 5 lb by dapping. Another thing is that many fish get off the hook, simply because the angler is not in so much control as he would be in dry-fly fishing. He finds it difficult to strike and set the hook at the right time:

Wind on a stillwater

Although lakes, lochs and reservoirs are generally called stillwater, there is nothing still about them. The principal motivator on these

Big dapping fly for seatrout on lochs.

waters is the wind. The successful trout angler appreciates this and knows how to use the wind to advantage, whether fishing from the bank or from a boat. Why? Because fish also use the wind to their advantage.

The first thing to remember about wind on a stillwater is that it usually dictates where the fish will be feeding. It may even influence how they are feeding. Although trout in rivers take up positions where their food is carried to them downstream, in still-waters they have to travel to find their food. And they travel where they know there will be the most insect life blowing from a certain direction.

When I first started fishing from a boat on stillwater I formed the notion myself that if the wind was blowing off a certain side of the lake, then that was the side in which I should be fishing. I even went further in my notion by using flies of a colour and pattern which roughly matched the colour and pattern of the land at that side of the water.

Of course all this was far too simplistic, and a bit naïve, but little though I knew it, my thoughts were approximately on the right lines. Fortunately, my study and knowledge of the subject has advanced considerably since those beginners' days. What I now know is that the wind can stir up the bottom and release feeding for the fish. Trout will stay in warmer water providing it has plenty of oxygen, and this is what wind does to the surface so that although some shallows may be warm, the trout will stay there until the wind goes away. Then they will go away.

Although having the wind at your back — either fishing from the bank or from a boat — is very satisfying for casting, it is better to have a side wind. Then you should use a floating line (or perhaps a line with a sinking tip) and either nymphs or slightly weighted flies. Cast across the wind and retrieve your flies slowly. What you are doing here is trying out various depths to see where the fish are feeding (because you can be sure they are feeding at some depth). Try a faster retrieve, then a slower one and so on until you hit a fish. If you do, keep casting again and again at this depth.

On a stillwater, particularly on a windy day, you will see 'wind lanes'. These are snaking 'roads' patterned on the surface of the water and caused by wind turbulence. Trout often feed on the edge of these lanes and, again trying out various depths, you should be lucky in regions like these.

Rainbow trout, unlike brown trout, tend to cruise in shoals in stillwaters, and you will often find that they travel in a sort of migration pattern, moving up against the wind and getting food from the surface or just beneath it as it is carried by that wind.

Look for the 'wind lanes' on a stillwater.

Again, to catch these fish, constantly testing the depth at which they are feeding is essential for success. A stillwater and the variable winds which come across it is the place for an angler to test his perseverance and patience by his willingness to change depth, pattern of flies, weight of flies and even the type of line he is using. Trout will change as the wind changes, and the angler must learn to do likewise.

All change on a stillwater

Trout anglers who fish from a boat are usually successful when they learn all the 'tricks of the trade'. They change tactics, change lines, change the depths at which they fish, and change direction, and this is why when they come ashore at the end of a day's session, their fish on the weighing-room table are usually bigger and there are more of theirs than the others.

What do the 'others' do? Well, they fish as I did for years until I got what I term a 'BGO' — a Blinding Glimpse of the Obvious — and I began to catch more and bigger trout. What is the Obvious? To me, it means simply that most of the time, trout on a lake don't 'go off'. Anglers who wait for a wind or wait for a rise or wait till the sun goes away might wait all week before realizing that waiting doesn't work.

A nice rainbow trout from Lartington Low Lake in Teesdale.

Trout — for the most part of the season — are feeding all the time *somewhere*. What the angler has to do is estimate where that 'somewhere' is, then change his methods to search for it. This could mean many things.

Flies
A change of flies seems the obvious thing to do when the fishing goes dead. But simply changing the pattern of flies, although the simplest procedure, is rarely the most successful. What is usually a better bet is a change of *size*, because trout may be shunning one size of insect at a certain time in favour of another, larger aquatic creature.

Line
This is often the most promising change in a dull period. Changing from a floater to a sinker (or vice versa) is usually the *first*

change employed by the experts. Then there are the types of line in between, like sinking tip etc.

Venue

It is quite possible that although the trout may be absent where *you* are fishing, they are somewhere else in the lake. This is particularly true with rainbows, because they tend to shoal and feed together anyway. Depending on the wind direction, they will go where there is the best chance of a meal. And this is where you have to think as a trout would.

Anchor

Particularly if you are fishing in a boat alone, the use of an anchor can be very good. You slip the anchor over the stern, fish for a time, then quietly raise the anchor off the bed of the lake, let the boat drift gently, lower the anchor again and resume fishing. This brings you to 'fresh' water every time.

Drogue

When there is a stiff wind on the lake, a drogue is essential if you don't want to be blown all over the place. I can remember once fishing alone in a boat on a Scottish Highland loch. I had no drogue and my day was ruined simply because by the time I had shut off my engine and unfastened my rod and tackle to start fishing, I was over on the other side of the loch! Two anglers in a boat nearby fished in comfort all day because they had had the sense to bring a drogue.

While I would never recommend impetuous or impatient angling on a boat, change is more necessary on a stillwater than on a river, simply because the angler on a river is constantly searching new lies and fresh areas. On a lake the fish tend to behave the same way all over.

Plumbing the depths for trout

There was a time when everybody who fly fished for salmon or trout used a line which floated. When fly fishing became popular as a sport for gentlemen in the eighteenth century, of course, the only line used was one tied to the tip of the rod. Reels were not yet invented and these lines were, in fact, the cast, or leader, to which was attached the artificial fly on the end. They were made of horsehair, either single strand or plaited.

Around 1885 anglers began using silk lines dressed with oil, because by that time reels had been invented and were used to carry more and more line. These lines all floated. The oil-dressed or greased line for salmon fishing is still used today by some anglers, and whole books have been written on fishing with greased line.

It was possibly an accident that caused the sinking line to be appreciated. Very likely some angler forgot to oil or grease his line and — surprise! — he caught fish. From that moment there has been a constant stream of different lines from manufacturers — the fast sinker, sinking tip etc. What has been increasingly realized by anglers — is that the depth at which trout feed varies according to conditions, and that this depth is all-important to the angler and the tackle he is using.

This appreciation of feeding depth is why some very good anglers catch fish galore, especially on stillwater, whereas others have a blank day. Too often there is no way of knowing the depth of the feeding fish on a particular day, or even at a particular hour. Surface activity can be deceiving. Those dimples and rings you see on the surface of a flat calm water might simply be signs of the trout nymphing, or getting the insects on their way *up* to the surface. Finding the depth of feeding fish is largely a matter of trial and error plus experience. But it is essential for catching fish. Flies can be cast over an area of water, sinking to a certain depth, and recovered hour after hour fruitlessly, because there are simply no fish feeding at that depth.

There are various ways of 'plumbing the depths', either on a lake or a river. You can fish with a floating line using small flies which have a heavy body. These will sink all right, but you have the advantage of seeing your line all the time. You can use ordinary wet flies and place tiny ball weights further up the leader. Or you can simply use a sinking line, or a fast-sinking line, or a lead-cored line. These days you can also buy a line with a sinking tip.

In addition to the use of various weights and types of fly and line, of course, you are in a position of controlling your flies yourself so that they reach approximately the depth of water you desire. If you are wet-fly fishing, it is obvious that the longer you pause once the flies are in the water, the deeper they will sink. Conversely, if you retrieve them quickly after reaching the water, you can be sure you are fishing just below the surface.

However you handle the problem of depth, be sure of one thing — fish do feed at various times. And much of your challenge as an angler is to estimate their dining area!

Use a mental check-list before you set out to fish from a boat.

Fishing from a boat

If there was ever any kind of fishing which requires the use of a check-list, even a mental one, it is fishing on a lake or a reservoir from a boat. The time to remember your waterproof over-trousers is not when you are a mile from the shore and caught in drenching rain. It is no use wondering how you can get a fish into the boat after you've forgotten to bring your landing net. And when the fuse-pin of your outboard engine is sheared because you steered the boat over some rocks in shallow water, it is too late to wish you had brought a spare. I know. I have made all these mistakes — and paid for them.

Anchor
When there is a stiff breeze and you find the boat drifting too fast for decent fishing, you will be glad of a good anchor and 30 yards of nylon rope. A hefty lump of concrete with a ring-bolt sunk in it does nicely.

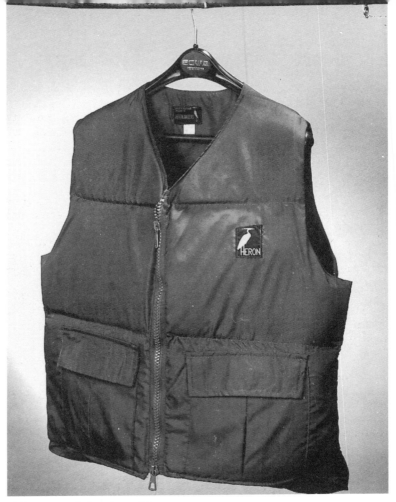

A buoyancy jacket for safety.

Drogue

We have examined the uses of a drogue earlier. This is an excellent 'water parachute' for slowing the boat in a wind and making the drift more manageable.

Rowlocks

If you lose an oar, which sometimes happens as a result of trying to get the oar into the 'U'-shaped rowlocks and occasionally when the rowlock itself is dislodged and falls into the water and sinks you can be in a pickle.

There is a simple way of preventing the rowlocks from dislodging and dropping over the side. At the bottom of the rowlock you will find a little hole. This is to accommodate a fastener, such as string, which in turn is tied to a spar on the seat. Or you can use a piece of fence-wire to go through the hole and keep the rowlock secure. Either way, string or wire, make sure each of your rowlocks is secured this way.

Buoyancy jacket
Some of the earlier life-jackets recommended by boat fishers, quite frankly, were not very practical. They were big, cumbersome and hindered the angler's casting.

This is not the case today with the new snug-fitting buoyancy jackets. They are worn like vests, have pockets for various items of tackle, and although not very bulky, they are guaranteed to keep a heavy person afloat for many hours.

The choice is yours whether you wear one or not. You should at least have in the boat flotation cushions (on some stillwaters it is mandatory to have these aboard) or some other life-saving item in case of disaster.

Changing seats
When the time comes for 'all change' and the person on the oars now has his spell at fishing, be *very* careful. If the water is choppy and the boat is rocking, pull ashore and make the change of seats there.

Food and refreshments
Don't take alcohol aboard. If you must have a beer or a dram, have it ashore. Remember to fasten your flask of coffee or tea securely and have your sandwiches well wrapped in a plastic bag.

Fishing the drift
The most common method of fly fishing is to let the boat drift gently down-wind (restrained by a drogue when necessary) and in this way you and your fellow angler are covering 'fresh' water each cast.

The thing to do is to quickly plan your drift, which you do by assessing the wind direction, judging whether you will need to put a drogue out or not, then positioning the boat as far up-wind as practical, so that you are casting in the direction of the bank. The most usual place for trout to cruise or feed is about twenty yards from the shore. Of course you must avoid bank anglers.

Cover the most likely places — sunk fences, headlands, quiet bays, weed beds. And look for 'wind lanes', the strips of quieter water between the turbulence of windswept surfaces. Trout often lie on the edge of these lanes.

The common method of casting from a boat is called 'loch-style', simply because it is the way many anglers on Scottish lochs fish for trout. Another term is 'short-lining', to differentiate it from the 'long-lining' method of casting a shooting-head or a reverse-taper line with a lure on the end of the leader, and hauling the line back so that the lure travels under the surface almost as a spinning lure might.

Here is how you fish 'loch-style'. You make casts of 10–15 yards only. Aim your team of three flies as if you want them to settle about a foot or so *above* the surface. In this way the flies will roll out gently, kiss the surface and sink. As soon as they do sink, raise your rod slightly and using your fingers on the line with your non-casting hand, draw the leader towards you so that the flies trip over the waves in a realistic manner. Then repeat the process.

Often the fish will have a go at the dropper, snatching it just before it breaks the surface. If this happens, lower your rod slightly so that the hook sets firmly in his mouth as he turns. Then raise the rod and play the fish until he is ready for the net.

As you cast, remember always that your fellow angler is also casting and try to alternate yours with his. And don't poach his water. Nothing irritates me more in a boat than a companion who casts his flies widely all over his own and my water selfishly. Some very inconsiderate anglers with whom I have fished have even stood up, and cast all round the boat! There are some *very* unsportsmanlike anglers around. Be sure you are not one of them.

Blundering about on a boat alarms the fish by the vibrations and possibly causes you and your companion to be irritated. The landing net should be placed so that both of you can get at it when necessary. And each haversack should be beside its owner, including the food and beverages. The usual number of anglers fishing from a boat is two, ideally with a third not fishing but guiding the boat gently with the oars. Unless it is a very large boat, three anglers fishing is too crowded for comfort, and is really inviting trouble — perhaps a hook in an ear!

Chapter 8

The time and the place

Is there an ideal time to fish for trout?

Opinions differ. Some anglers prefer the brisk days of spring, others the bee-droning afternoons of summer. Each to his taste on trout fishing, but if you were to ask me to describe my ideal conditions for fishing wet-fly for trout, I would say something like this.

First, I would be on a river. The water-level would be just right — not coloured, but gin-clear and running off after a few days' rain. I would be standing on a pebble shore in front of a brisk, streamy part of the river just where the white water was beginning to fan outwards in pleasant swirls and reaching the far bank which is overhung with pleasant trees and bushes, and I would know that under them would be lying one or two big 'grandfather' fish calmly taking in passing flies or grub or insects, while their younger offspring pranced about at the end of the pool midstream. And I would think that a few more of those bigger fish would be lying quietly feeding at the very end of the pool.

It would be a light, pleasant day in early summer, not too bright and certainly not thundery (in my experience thundery weather puts the trout off). There would be a gentle breeze at my back, helping me to cast out evenly and sweetly. It would be a dependable little wind, not one of those erratic things that comes in gusts and upsets every third or fourth cast. And there would be some cloud in the sky, enough to screen any sudden impudent blaze of sunshine.

The time of the day would be such that I was facing most of the light, so that I could follow the cast of my flies, seeing exactly where they were falling into the stream and where a trout might accept one of them — preferably that Greenwell's Glory on the tail!

This unusual bridge on a reservoir is an ideal casting platform.

I would then wade out gently, not too far, and make my first cast. Nothing. Then I would wait, peer into the stream to see signs of fish feeding, possibly see a tell-tale ring erupting then disappearing downstream. A fish! Where? Exactly where the ring *started*. And if I am very careful, very cautious with my next cast, maybe I can have him!

I peel off more line gently, take a couple of preliminary casts to straighten out the line, then settle my flies lightly just above where I think I saw that ring.

Chug!

Missed him! What happened? I don't know. Maybe he spat the fly out. Maybe I struck, too rapidly, instead of raising the rod in one gentle rhythmic movement. I would try again. And with luck this time he would be mine.

Somehow the 'ideal' conditions are easier to assess on a loch. And, above anything, a wind is a great advantage on a stillwater.

Without wind on a lake, trout fishing can be a dull, uninspiring exercise and I have known such 'blank' times day after day, especially in high summer. Nothing beats a good rippling wave on a loch. The artificiality of your flies is better concealed, and you can move them a little to give them life in addition to the normal retrieval. Results speak for themselves — far more trout are caught in lochs on windy days rather than on calm ones. As on a river, I prefer to be facing the light so that I can follow each cast with my eyes better. I dislike casting into gloom or shade.

I must say, however, that regardless of whether I am fishing a river or a loch, the 'bonanza' time for me is the twilight. That rosy late-evening period is a joy to fish, not only because it conceals the deception of my flies better, but simply because that's when the bigger fish feel bolder and come out to feed more brazenly. Many a two and three-pound trout has paid dearly for their over-confidence at that time on a summer evening!

As darkness deepens, I change my cast of flies for bigger ones, and in summer and I have often fished all through the night. For some reason, there is usually a 'blank' period in night fishing when there is nothing doing at all. In July this is often between 11.30 p.m. and 1.30 a.m. Then towards 2.00 a.m., as the first dim light of dawn is starting, the fun starts. From then on till full morning light, in my estimation, is the very best of summer trouting.

Fish safely

All sorts of serious accidents can happen to anglers, especially beginners. It has been said that angling is 'the contemplative man's sport'. Therefore how surprising it is to read newspaper accounts of anglers drowning in lakes and in the sea, sometimes in rivers, to say nothing of falls and bruises and misplaced hooks in ears and eyes. It requires more than contemplation to achieve these deaths and injuries; it takes carelessness or foolhardiness or both.

Here are some of the hazards you may encounter when fishing in a river:

Rising water

In heavy rain a river can rise rapidly. Depending on the nature of the river bed upstream, a spate after a downpour in one river may be quite different from that on another. Some rivers can rise

so rapidly that a wading angler may be thrown off-balance, or have to scramble for safety in the face of an onslaught of water.

The same thing can happen where a river is controlled by the outflow from a dam upstream. If the sluices are open, a torrent of water may come down-river very fast.

It is advisable to mark the height of the water with a stick or a stone, and refer to it occasionally. There is an additional advantage in knowing if a river is rising or falling, in that it gives a guide to the behaviour of the fish. Trout feed well in falling water, but will often 'go off' in a river which is beginning to rise. Why? It is my opinion that they know when a spate is on the way and — well, why bother with flies when worms and other insects are on the way?

Wading

Wading in a strange river has obvious dangers. The banking may be shelved, with a precipitous drop under the surface further out. There may be deep holes of which you are unaware. There may be shifting sands or gravel.

The answer? Use a wading stick and prod the bed carefully before each step.

Don't stand on rocks when casting. Stand between them. And when making progress across rocks, use your wading stick to maintain your balance. Many rocks are weed-covered and slippery.

Don't be tempted to wade into a current which you feel may be too fast. If you *do* wade into a speedy current, again use your wading stick.

A wading stick is an excellent 'extra' leg. Using it is like having three legs, only one of which should be lifted at a time when stepping. The stick should be about 3½ feet long, with a 'Y' top for grasping. It can be fastened with a lanyard to your belt or your haversack so that it cannot be lost.

If you feel in doubt about the depth of water in front of you, don't continue. In trout rivers the deepest parts are often between the middle of the river and the far bank where it drops steeply. Indeed that is where the trout usually lie. You can reach these feeding trout by skilful casting from a safe wading position, rather than trying to wade into their territory. Indeed, you will stand a better chance of catching a trout this way.

If you must wade across a river, do so by wading across and upstream against the flow. Lean slightly against the flow to prevent yourself being swept downstream.

If you do fall into the water

If you miss your footing while wading, or if you fill your waders with water, or if you simply topple over by the force of the current, try to remember these points:

- Don't panic. Let go your rod.
- Keep your mouth shut.
- Hold your head back in the water.
- Keep your arms by your side.
- Let the current carry you downstream feet first so that your head will not hit rocks.
- Use your arms gently to steer you into calm water.
- Do not try to stand. *Crawl* out.
- Get warm and dry as quickly as possible and hope that you remembered to carry some spare clothes in the car.

Fishing at night

It may be some time before you decide to fish in the deep glow of evening or at night. One of the perversities of angling for trout (particularly seatrout) is that that is when the Big Boys come out to feed. And that's when a skilful and cautious angler stands the best chance of some thrilling fishing with excellent results.

It is also the time — on a river particularly — when the sport can be least comfortable and most hazardous. Before you go trekking off to the river one dark night, just think what you are getting into.

You park your car somewhere safe off the road. You set up your rod and tackle by the light of your headlights. You fiddle around with the selection of flies. Then, at long last thinking you have everything — rod, net, haversack, wading stick — you switch off the car headlights.

Blackness.

You don't know where you are. The familiar path to the river, which you know so well in daytime — where is it now?

Wait till your eyes get used to the darkness. Then you will spot the path and walk along it to the water. You wade in at the edge of the river very carefully, unfasten your tail-fly from the little bottom ring on your rod and start to peel off line, casting carefully.

That *can* be the picture for a beginner. I have been part of that picture many times when I started fishing, and I paid little attention to the dangers I was running.

Here are some tips if you wish to fish at night safely:

- Inspect the place where you want to fish by *daylight*, before you prepare for night fishing. Look where you may wade safely, note the speed of the water, the nature of the river bed. Are there any pot-holes? Any steep shelves? Any deep mud?
- Slow down all your movements when fishing at night. Step warily, carefully. Cast gently and remember that a long cast is rarely necessary at night. The fish may be almost at your feet!
- Set up your tackle in daylight and if you are driving to the river, use a couple of rod carriers on the roof of your car.
- Mark your fly boxes and any other important items of tackle with luminous tape.
- Carry a torch.
- *Don't* lay anything down on the bank. You may never find it at night.
- *Don't* fish alone. Go along with someone, preferably someone who knows the water well

On a fishing trip you can drown, lose your life, break a limb, or lose an eye with a mis-cast hook. The least thing that might happen to you is to fill your waders, get soaked and have your outing ruined. There *is* an alternative, though, and that is to fish safely, with the right equipment.

Mark your fly box with luminous tape.

Fishing from a boat

- Don't go out on a lake in a boat unless you are wearing, or have instant access to, a buoyancy jacket.
- Don't go out at all if the boatman or the fishery manager or the hotel manager advises against it.
- Don't fish in waters too far from the shore if you are a stranger to them.

Remember that outboard engines, even the best of them, need some expertise in operating them, and if you get stuck miles from anywhere and a strong wind springs up, you could be in trouble. Check everything before you set off — oars, rowlocks, fuel for the engine, spare plug and the state of the boat itself.

If there are three in a boat — say, two fishing and one steadying the boat by the oars — make sure you arrange who fishes at the stern and who at the bow. Under these circumstances, one person will have to cast over the left-hand shoulder. Can he do it? Is he also a beginner? Or — blessed day! — is he a left-handed person? If both of you are beginners, make quite sure that there is no danger of 'hooking' each other, or the person at the oars.

Don't stand up. More drowning accidents in small boats are caused by this foolishness than anything else. One of my friends lost his life this way. He stood up in a windy day on a Scottish loch and he was wearing waders. Result? He toppled over, the boat capsized and his waders filled, sending him straight to the bottom. The other two anglers with him escaped drowning by the skin of their teeth.

Fishing a river

Don't wade a river unless you know it very well. If it is a strange river, or if you cannot see quite plainly where you are stepping, always use a wading stick. These have saved many a potential stumble and soaking. Here's another tip. Fasten a little circular-headed screw on to the wading stick, fix a cord to it and tie the cord on to your belt or haversack. If you drop the stick to cast and fish, you can be sure that the stick will simply float near your feet and be held by the cord from drifting downstream.

Breast waders are rarely if ever used fishing for trout. Frankly I don't like them, even fishing for salmon. If the possibility of wading out of your depth and filling your thigh-length waders is hazardous, just think what might happen if you stumbled and fell in a strong current wearing chest waders! Yes, I know that some

This boat at Bayham Lake is anchored and probably quite safe. However, as a rule anglers should not stand up in boats.

experts demonstrate what you should do in chest waders if you topple over. For my part, I would rather not try!

Fishing in a remote area

What do you imagine is the dominant danger in fishing on a lovely moorland or a hill stream or a remote lake in the middle of nowhere? Is it the danger of getting lost? Or forgetting to take a compass? Or being trapped in a mountain mist?

You will be surprised to know that the big hazard in such places is being electrocuted. Already some anglers have been killed by electricity in wilderness areas; some of them indeed in non-wilderness areas.

It works like this. In some parts of the country — usually far away from towns and villages — the authorities have built electricity pylons with overhead power lines which are surprisingly low where the ground rises up towards the pylon. The result is that these power lines are in many instances only a short distance above the head of any person walking under them.

One of the most likely people to be under such lines is an angler, perhaps fishing a moorland burn or a river in an unpopulated part of the countryside. And if the angler is using a carbon-fibre rod and in casting his line touches the overhead cable — that's that. He will be at the receiving end of thousands of volts.

This is why the electricity boards issue notices for display in fishing tackle shops saying 'Look up!' A wet fishing line and a carbon-fibre rod are ideal carriers of electricity — and very, very lethal.

Fish alone or with others

Really, what kind of fish you angle for depends to a large extent on the kind of person you are, where you want to be and, above everything, with *whom* you want to be.

Broadly, there are two kinds of fishermen: the 'loners' and the 'clubby' people. Don't ask me to offer a preference, because I have enjoyed both experiences: I have fished alone on wild,

Life jackets are compulsory on Queen Mother Reservoir.

remote moorland lochs: and I have joined a cheery group of anglers in a coach off to a river or loch. I have also fished competitively, had holidays in fishing hotels, been out in a boat with one or two friends, and fished all week on my own.

All right — I *will* offer a personal preference. For me, nothing is more enjoyable than a few days' fishing with a friend who knows how to keep quiet, knows how to keep to his own chosen stretch of water, but who is good, chatty company back in the car at lunch-time.

Not everyone likes such sparse company, however. Indeed, among the three million or so anglers in Britain, you may be sure that the majority of these go for their outings with clubs, and their ideal fishing day is to line up along a river bank with scores of their mates — or go out to sea in a boat with twenty others.

For these reasons, I must offer the opinion that trout fishing is more suitable for the angler who likes to fish either alone, or at most with a few other anglers. 'Mass' trout fishing is almost a contradiction in terms. To the dry-fly purist or the otherwise *real* enthusiast, it is unthinkable.

Really it is my wife who is the best advocate for game fishing — and for trout fishing in particular. No, she does not fish, but listen to what she said to me one glorious summer day, sitting on the bank of the Spey five miles upstream from Grantown when we were having our lunch under a tree and there was the chequerboard pattern of the sunshine through the leaves.

'D'you know, I've just realized something. If you didn't fish on rivers like this and I didn't come with you, what other opportunity would we have to come to a waterside?'

'You don't think we'd come here for a picnic anyway?'

'Not really. We might *want* to — but how would we know where to go? And besides the picnic itself, what reason would we have?'

'You mean my fishing gives us a purpose in being here?'

'Yes. And those other places we've been to — the hill lochs and being out in that boat yesterday evening and up on those moors last Monday.'

Don't imagine it is only an angler's wife who enjoys the surroundings that come with trout fishing. If you go after this wily fish and have an eye for scenic beauty at all, all the rest of your surroundings will be a great bonus — hopefully for your family as well as yourself.

Then there is the wildlife — the vegetation, the birds and the animals. I am sure it is wise editorial discretion which causes many of our fishing magazines to feature a regular little write-up and a picture of the various birds and other wildlife creatures we meet on a fishing trip. Anglers, particularly trout anglers, like to feel at one with nature on their outings.

I have fished rivers in the Scottish Highlands and had a deer at sunset quietly drinking at a pool only fifty yards upstream from me. I have made friends with little birds around my fishing hut while having my lunch. Birds of the mountain and moorland are never far away in some of these wild places where the trout abound. I have fished with equal pleasure in a quiet chalk-stream in pastoral, tree-lined river banks fringed with flowers.

So there is the bonus for the trout fisher. No wonder Izaak Walton called it 'the contemplative man's sport'.

When to join a club

There is one important difference between angling clubs and other kinds of clubs like golf or badminton or bowling. Joining is not at all essential. There are as many anglers who are 'loners' as there are 'clubby' ones.

Some anglers like to fish hotel waters, some like to fish entirely on their own on private beats, and others simply buy the occasional ticket from a local association to fish its waters. These people are not 'joiners', and indeed shy away from others when they fish.

For all this, joining a club is an excellent idea if you are a beginner, providing you like the company of others. There are many other benefits. Somebody will teach you to fish: indeed some clubs retain the services of a professional angler for this purpose. Many clubs own or lease their own waters — rivers or lakes — and by joining, you are guaranteed a fishing outing when you like. As a rule, membership fees are not at all high (except perhaps in a few of those very exclusively dry-fly clubs whose chalk-streams and other waters are carefully and expensively preserved).

Winter time, when the trout season is over, is active too, in a typical club. You will be invited to get-togethers, video shows, lectures and discussions on all kinds of piscatorial subjects. Fly-tying instruction and exhibitions of rods and equipment pass the dark evenings excellently until the glorious opening day in spring.

But it is the spirit of competition that sustains most angling clubs. The members — not unlike golf clubs — run contests throughout the season, either on their own water or somebody else's. Prizes, some of them surprisingly valuable, are presented to the person with the biggest catch of the day, or the heaviest fish. All in all, club members, in my experience, are the most agreeable, cheerful, companionable people you are likely to find.

A get-together of anglers at the Lake of Menteith in Scotland.

Fishing is no sport for the disgruntled or the miserable, especially in the company of others. All this has something to do with the nature of angling, to say nothing of everyone being together on a river bank or out in a boat on a lake. If you doubt this, pick up any fishing magazine and look at the smiles on the faces of club members in a group photograph.

You should join a club at one of two stages in your angling life — at the very beginning, when you know little or nothing about the sport, or later when you get fed up fishing on your own and having difficulty finding good fishing water.

However you decide, I would recommend that you support your club loyally, attend the meetings — even the business ones, which are often hilarious, and certainly the annual dinner which is *always* hilarious.

There are hundreds of angling clubs all over the the country catering for all types of fishermen — sea anglers, salmon anglers, dry-fly 'purists', coarse fishermen, and even some 'specialist' ones whose members fish for one type of fish only, such as pike.

If you want to join a club, choose one well. As a trout angler you will want one that preferably has its own water and whose members fish for trout with, perhaps, the occasional day on a salmon or seatrout river.

Tying your own flies

There will come a time, sooner or later, when you will want to catch trout with flies you have tied yourself. Fly-tying in winter evenings for some anglers is a hobby in itself. For others, particularly dry-fly fishers, it can be an obsessive pastime as engrossing as angling itself. This is understandable. What greater thrill can you have than catching a trout which you have been stalking and feel it pull on the very fly you have tied yourself?

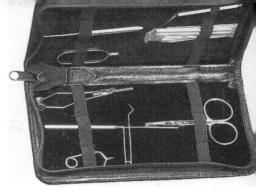

Tying flies at a bench. *A small portable fly-tying outfit.*

In some areas there are fly-tying evening classes, and if there is one in your neighbourhood, I would recommend that you join it. If not, you can teach yourself the skill with the help of a book on the subject from your local library. One of the best I know is *Flyfishing* by Brian Furzer, in which there is a simple-to-follow chapter.

Here are the tools and material you need for tying flies:

Vice	A movable table lamp
Hooks	A plastic box to store the flies
Bobbin holder	Thread
Pliers	Varnish
Scissors	Range of feathers
Dubbing needle	Range of fur hair
Wax	Range of silks

All of these can be purchased at your fishing tackle shop. With the exception of dry flies, whose similarity to the real insect must be precise, never forget that flies for fishing wet downstream, and lures, are frequently attractors, and need not be exact replicas of

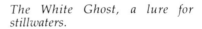

An effective dry fly — the Black Gnat. *The White Ghost, a lure for stillwaters.*

the real flies. For example, I have yet to see a *real* Black Zulu fly, yet I have caught many trout and seatrout with the tied version.

In tying a wet fly you are making it to sink. Therefore some — sometimes all — of the body has tinsel wound round it. The wings slope back over the business-end of the hook.

Conversely, dry flies are made to float, so the wings can slope any way and the body is usually sparsely dressed.

A lure, like the wet fly, is made to sink, but it is larger and is intended to imitate some tiny minnow or other water creature travelling under the surface in jerking movements.

Be a sport!

Angling has its rules, plenty of them. Some are laid down by law, like no fishing without permission. Some are rules drawn up by the local club or association or fishery. But there are others, really laid down by no one, yet understood between anglers — a code of practice, you might say. And if you ignore these you will be very unpopular, perhaps even banned or asked to leave the club or association or the fishery. Generally this 'code' is called sportsmanship.

On a river

- If you are fishing a good pool with likely prospects of catching trout, don't hog it. If there is another angler waiting to follow you through the pool, don't dawdle! 'A cast and a step' downstream is the understanding. Respect the wishes of other anglers.
- Keep your advice to yourself unless it is asked for. Proffering unwanted suggestions about what fly to use etc. is very disagreeable to some anglers, particularly if they come from a novice!
- In the same vein, never shout advice to another angler if he is playing a fish.
- Never tie another angler's knots or — unless he desperately asks — net his fish.
- Be as quiet and unobtrusive as possible when another angler is fishing.
- Don't disturb another angler's water.
- Take care when you are casting. Make sure nobody is behind.

On a lake

- As on a river, where there are other anglers — 'a cast and a step'.
- Wade from the bank disturbing the water as little as possible.
- If you wish to anchor your boat, don't do so in the middle of the best drifts on the lake.
- If there are three of you in a boat, two fishing and one on the oars, make sure you take your turn at the agreed time.
- Don't disturb the water in front of another drifting boat.
- Don't use your outboard if it disturbs other anglers fishing.
- If you are on the oars and guiding the boat on a drift, do so quietly and steadily.

Anywhere

- Don't leave litter; pick it up and take it home.
- If you are permitted access to a water through a farmer's land, respect his property.
- Close all gates behind you.
- Don't park your car anywhere on private property unless you have permission.
- Don't block access to property.
- Don't light fires.

Look after your tackle

Fishing tackle does not take care of itself. Buying it is one thing; making sure that it works properly every time and that it lasts its proper life-span is another.

Bill Howes catches some early season rainbows.

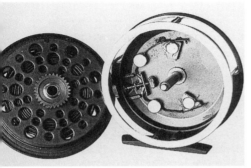

Above *Salt water, even diluted can be very corrosive.*

Above left *Clean your reel before the start of the season.*

Left *Replace faulty rod rings.*

Rod
Wipe it down after a fishing trip. And if by any chance you have been fishing in salt or brackish water — this is quite possible on the estuary of a river, for example — make sure you wash all your equipment thoroughly in fresh water, then dry it before packing it away. Sea-water, even diluted estuary water, can be very corrosive.

Line
At least once a year, preferably at the start of the season, strip off your line and clean it with a fly-line cleaner which the tacklist will stock. Then check the backing to make sure there are no weak spots.

Reel
Most of today's fly reels come apart quite easily for cleaning and oiling, and this should be done before the start of the season.

Waders
It is easy enough these days to purchase a pair of metal clamps which you fix to the soles of your waders before hanging them upside down to air and dry.

Rod rings
Rod rings are important to the life and efficiency, of your line. Why? Because if any of the rings develops corrosion on the inside, this will constantly wear and tear the line. Examine the rings at the start of the season and replace any faulty ones.

Flies
The hooks on artificial flies rust. Sometimes the rust is almost invisible, especially on bushy flies where the hook is hidden. Any that show signs of even the slightest corrosion should be thrown away, otherwise you may lose a good fish when the hook breaks.

Net
If your landing net is one of the flip-out kind, make sure at the start of the season that it *does* flip out. The time to realize that it has jammed is not when you are about to net a fish!

Waterproof jacket
Does it leak anywhere? Repair it.

The tried and trusted flies

One of my angling friends lives and fishes in the far north of Scotland. His angling playgrounds are the wonderful hill lochs, which are brimming with wild brown trout. He is an acknowledged expert in loch fishing for trout in his part of the world. Therefore, as you can imagine, visitors to his area constantly ask him about the flies he uses. They are amazed when he tells them that for *his* waters at any rate, he uses the same three flies and never varies them. One of them, of course, is a March Brown.

Whatever you may think of this frugality with flies, whether you put it down to laziness, or vanity, or plain ignorance, you can take my word for it that he catches his more-than-fair share of trout on these wilderness waters.

While I would never have the nerve or the blind faith to stick to three tried-and-true fly patterns through the whole season on

different waters, I must say that on wet-fly fishing at any rate, the thought of carrying in my kit a fly box crammed with every conceivable pattern and size makes me shudder. While I do advocate change when you feel it is necessary, an angler can become obsessed about variety of flies, and may spend more time matching them than fishing!

I am often asked (particularly by anglers' relatives as it gets near Christmas) if I will write down the names of artificial flies, so that they can be bought for the unsuspecting angler as a gift. Frankly, in the face of such ignorance of the subject, I could I suppose, give the names of half a dozen good old stand-bys and leave it at that. But that would really be a disservice these days, when some anglers fish nearby rivers, some reservoirs and others both. Really, recommending 'all round' flies is almost an impossibility.

Yet it must be said that some of the 'stand-bys' do catch fish regularly, and are recognized as winners. For beginners who have yet to develop their knowledge and become fastidious about selecting flies, or who have yet to tie their own patterns, here are some tried-and-trusted flies which are very suitable most of the time on many waters:

Wet flies for brown trout on rivers

March Brown	Black Palmer
Greenwell's Glory	Grouse and Claret
Woodcock and Yellow	Jock Scott
Butcher	Peter Ross
Olive Quail	

Wet flies for lakes and stillwaters

Teal and Green	Wickham's Fancy
Black Pennel	Partridge and Yellow

Artificial nymphs

Shrimp	Blue Dun
Black Buzzer	Iron Blue Dun
Olive	Bloodworm

Dry flies for trout on rivers

Black Gnat	Grey Duster
The Last Hope	John Storey
Humpy	Black Buzzer

Reservoir flies and lures

Baby Doll
Muddler Minnow
Jack Frost

Sweeney Todd
Badger Matuka
Ace of Spades

Seatrout flies on rivers

Blue Zulu
Black Zulu
Alexandra

Bloody Butcher
Dunkeld
Cinnamon and Gold

Chapter 9

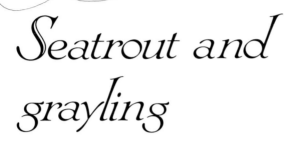

Seatrout and grayling

The seatrout

There are two things you should know about seatrout which, strangely, seem to contradict each other. The first is that the sea trout is the same species as the brown trout, except that it migrates to the sea and then returns to its home river. The second is that in strict terms of the law, it is considered the same as salmon. This simply means that the owner of a seatrout river has certain rights of conservancy, as he would for salmon. The distinction between that and for brown trout need not bother you much, except that the permit to fish a seatrout water is usually included in the salmon ticket, and therefore costs more.

The identification of the seatrout as simply the migrating type of *Salmo trutta* is fairly recent. It was originally thought to be a separate species. Scientific opinion now is that both are the same species. For all this, as an angler, you will find great differences in behaviour between the brown trout and the seatrout. Indeed there was a time in recent history when the seatrout was called a salmon-trout, and there are some uninformed people even today who use that term.

Seatrout usually begin their spawning in October or November, and sometimes go on right through the winter. Like the salmon, they prefer a gravel bed in the river (these spawning areas, by the way, are called 'redds') but unlike their bigger cousins, they like shallower water and finer gravel. Sometime they will spawn in a depth of water which barely covers their backs.

About a hundred days elapse before the eggs are ready to hatch; then, as baby fish, they go to the estuary of the river and swim backwards and forwards with the ebb and flow of the tide. After a few months of this, feeding and growing all the time, they

The late Bill McEwan, famed Loch Lomond angler, with a seatrout of 12½lb and some smaller bretheren.

go to the sea in the spring, then return in the summer and autumn to the river. As virgin seatrout coming into the river to mate and spawn for the first time, they are known by different names in various parts of the country — finnock, whitling, herling, sewin, sprod or peal. Their usual weight is about half-a-pound, and many anglers fish for them enthusiastically.

Since some seatrout, particularly in Irish, Welsh and Scottish rivers, grow to weights of four or five pounds (and there is record of some eighteen pounds being caught) it is perhaps understandable why the law classes the seatrout as salmon. And it is also understandable why some anglers who may catch a big seatrout have difficulty differentiating it from a salmon, because they do look alike to the inexperienced eye. The main clue to the difference is in the tail. In the salmon the tail is slightly forked. Even when you stretch it, the forked shape still shows. In the seatrout the tail is almost square. In addition, the 'wrist' part of the tail is different, as you will soon know if you try to land your fish by gripping it on this part. If it is a salmon, you stand a reasonable chance of landing your fish and taking him by this grip up the bank. If it is a seatrout, the chance of doing so are minimal; the fish will slip through your hand no matter how firmly you try to hold it.

Unlike the salmon, most of which migrate into fresh water only once then die as kelts (spent fish), the seatrout will come into rivers as often as ten times during its life. Some fish of over 20 lb have been caught in Britain, and in Scandinavia some of the largest seatrout in the world have been caught.

Fishing for seatrout

First find your water. Seatrout rivers in most countries are not in abundant supply these days. There are plenty in Scandinavia, but in Britain the good rivers for this fish are mainly in Ireland, Wales and Scotland. And, of course, there are the lochs in Scotland and the loughs in Ireland.

Happily for the holiday angler, most of the seatrout runs, certainly in Scotland and in many of the other 'seatrout' areas in Europe — occur in June and July, with a hold-over into August in some cases.

The rod I would suggest for seatrout fishing is like that for the brown trout — nine or ten feet, with a No. 7 double-tapered line and a nylon leader of five or six lb breaking strain. In spite of the fact that some angling books casually refer to wet-fly fishing for seatrout with a cast of three flies as for brown trout, I always fish with two flies only, a tail-fly and a dropper. The first time you hook a seatrout, particularly a hefty one of around three or four lb, will soon show you why. A three-fly cast is difficult to handle when a savagely fighting seatrout is on one of the hooks. The other two flies are all over the place, and should one of them catch hold of a branch or a stone, you can be sure Mr Seatrout will feel the opportunity and break off the fly on which he is impaled.

The favourite time for fishing for seatrout on a river is in the deep dusk or at night. Remember that the prime season for them is usually June and July, so fishing at night is not so uncomfortable or difficult as it might be earlier or later in the season. For all this, night or deep-evening fishing *does* have its hazards — deep holes in the river bed, shifting gravel, slippery rocks. All of these might seem innocuous enough by day. By night, believe me, they are magnified out of all proportion. It is for these reasons that I recommend a thorough reconnaissance of the water by daytime beforehand. And remember to take a wading stick and a torch.

Night fishing for seatrout does have wonderful advantages for an angler who appreciates a natural, unspoilt environment. The night bird-calls, the purple silhouette shapes of trees and rocks, the gentle gurgling of the river — all these make for tranquillity of mind and an unforgettable experience with nature.

Remember what you have learned about the habitat and feeding habits of the brown trout. Those of the seatrout are not much different when it comes to territory and concealment and ease of feeding — usually at the ends of pools on the river and within a few yards at the most from the refuge of a bank overhung with bushes or a tree. Fish gently, fish in deadly quietness, fish slowly and with infinite patience. Then wait for that pull on your line and raise your rod steadily to set the hook in his mouth.

Fishing at night for seatrout, you should never try to disentangle a cast. Reel in, walk away from the water, then by the light of your torch simply take off the tangled cast, put it away safely and tie on a new cast which you have already prepared against this eventuality. Tangles you will have, be under no doubt, because you are fishing 'blind' much of the time and you are fishing near trees and bushes, the distance of which is very difficult to gauge in darkness. One further thing about changing casts: make sure that the beam from your torch does not shine on the water.

What flies for the seatrout?

There are some anglers who think that because seatrout take an artificial fly (especially at night) so ferociously, and because they

Above *Essential for night fishing — wading stick and torch.*

Right *What fly next?*

fight so strongly, it is a fish which must feed voraciously in a river. This is not so.

The life-cycle of the seatrout is much the same as for salmon, but whereas the salmon does not feed at all in fresh water, the seatrout does *occasionally*. It certainly does not get sufficient feeding to sustain it all the time during its spawning run. Mostly it is sustained by the tissue and fat built up while it was feeding at sea.

As far as you are concerned, the important word is 'occasionally'. It is as well for the angler's sake that it does. Unlike the insect food of the brown trout, however, the seatrout is more attracted to those which represent its main diet while it is at sea — small fish like sand-eels, pilchards and sprats. This does not mean that it will not be attracted to the same kinds of artificial fly used for brown trout. What it does mean is that such flies are of a different type. The small fish-life to which the seatrout is accustomed range from tiny things of ¼ inch up to 3 inches. Thus you can use tiny seatrout flies of size 14 or even 16, up to large three-hook feathered lures around 3 inches.

The main difference, however, apart from size, are the patterns. Well-known and successful seatrout flies are Silver Wilkinson (no relationship to the author), the Blue or Black Zulu, the Bloody Butcher and the Connemara. Most good seatrout flies have a glint of silver or gold about them, although I must confess that the best night's seatrout fishing I ever had in my life was on the Deveron river in Banff in Scotland, when I used a small size 12 Stoat's Tail with no glitter at all. The seatrout is a perverse creature!

A well-established method for catching seatrout is by fly-and-maggot, when a little maggot is fixed to the tail-fly. The only trouble I have found here is the difficulty in keeping the maggot on the fly, as it too frequently snaps off on the back cast.

Whether you use a large fish-imitation as a lure, or a small double-hooked fly, depends on many things — the time of day or night, the height of the water, the temperature, but mainly the season of the year. Early in the season a big fly is often best, for instance.

Other ways of catching seatrout

Fly fishing is by no means the only method of angling for seatrout. Spinning and bait fishing, or using lures, are very productive in the right conditions, although I must confess fly fishing to my mind is more satisfying and engages more skill.

Spinning

The best kind of spinning bait for seatrout, in my opinion, is a little Mepps spoon. It can be fished when the river is quite high and when the seatrout are in the white water or lurking under trees just out of the main current. Cast it slightly upstream of where you think the fish may be lying, let it tumble down through the rougher water and wait for the fish to dart out from its refuge to snatch it. Then raise your rod steadily and the rest is up to your judgement and skill.

Worm fishing

Under the right conditions on a big water, even coloured after a heavy spate, worm fishing can be even more productive. Cast the worm, preferable on a Stewart Tackle of three hooks, into the current, let it drift downstream gently, wait till it stops, and be ready to tighten up your line when you feel the 'chug-chug' of a seatrout taking the worm.

Right *The Mepps spoon.*

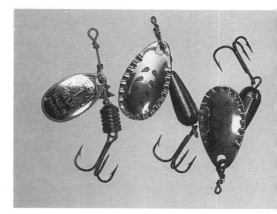

Below *A three-hook feathered lure for seatrout.*

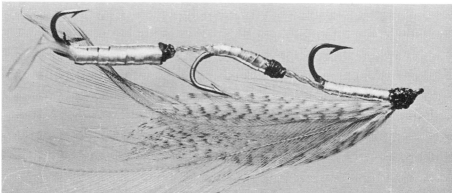

Top *Catch grayling at a different time of the year.*
Above *High time for grayling fishing is winter.*

Lure fishing

This is really fly fishing with a big tandem, feathered lure. In some
areas they call them Terrors. Night time has the most successful

potential here, preferably just before dawn in high summer, and it is the bigger fish that are attracted. When you feel the fish take the lure gently, don't hesitate. Strike it strongly and firmly.

The grayling

You might wonder why I have included a piece about a fish called the grayling in a book about trout fishing. The reason is simple. You catch grayling in almost the same way as you do the trout; but you catch them at a different time of the year. As the grayling spawns at a different time to the trout, they come into their prime when autumn is becoming winter, and this is why some anglers call them the winter trout. More commonly, the fish is called 'the lady of the stream' because of its graceful shape and colouring and the attractiveness of its high dorsal fin.

The grayling inhabits the same type of river as trout, and on some waters the fishing associations and owners net the fish to get them out of the water and transfer them to other waters. The reason for this is the general belief that grayling compete with trout for food, and these riparian owners who have valuable trout stretches don't like grayling among them, even in the close season.

There is a belief that grayling were introduced to waters in Britain from mainland Europe by monks, to ensure that there were always fish available on Fridays. Another, more dramatic story, is that when the British Isles separated from the rest of Europe, the grayling was the freshwater fish which went with them and that this is why grayling frequent rivers in the east of Britain but not the west. Frankly, I take both stories with a pinch of salt!

Fishing for grayling can be just as challenging and exciting as for trout. You use the same types of fly and the same methods. the 'take' by a grayling is usually sudden and explosive at the start, then it tends to slacken off as you bring it to the net.

By comparison with trout, the grayling has larger scales and is slimmer, and although it is an excellent fish for the table, the flesh is flaked much more that the trout's.

The reason why many enthusiastic trout anglers like the grayling is simply because when the trout season ends, they can carry on right through winter fishing for grayling. Indeed, grayling fishing in the snow is not unusual for some fishers who simply cannot put away their rods when trout fishing is over for the year.

Like rainbow trout, grayling tend to feed and move in shoals around the ends of pools on a river. For this reason you have to be very cautious in your movements as, if you scare one, you will scare them all at that spot.

Chapter 10

The big league

Get ready for your once-in-a-lifetime trout

As a trout angler you can be sure of one thing: sooner or later you will catch a monster. Don't forget that fish don't know whether the person at the other end of the fishing rod is an ignorant beginner or an expert. It's all the same to the trout, and this means big as well as small ones.

Of course, no one can deny that if it *is* a big fish you are after, you can do right things and wrong things to increase or decrease your chances of a monster. For instance, what is the sense of fishing some hill loch for a monster if no fish over ¾ lb has ever been caught on that water? So:

● Rule No 1: If you want a big trout, go where you know the big trout *are*.
● Rule No 2: Fish for big trout with a fly or a lure which attract the big ones.
● Rule No 3: Find out how other anglers catch big fish, and more or less do what they do — and fish when they fish.

A trout hooked on a Persuader lure on a stillwater.

It might interest you to know what I mean by a 'big trout'. The usual weight of a brown trout from a lake or a river is in the region of ½ lb to 1 lb. There are more fish of that size than bigger fish. The same might apply to rainbow trout, except that they grow faster and therefore there are more of the bigger size in a lake, particularly if the owners or managers have a stocking policy geared towards producing 'jumbos'. Indeed, some anglers go to certain lakes and reservoirs simply because there are big fish in them. In Canada and the USA, such fish are in a class by themselves and are called 'trophy' fish, and the lakes they inhabit are called 'trophy lakes'.

In Britain, some real monsters are being caught by expert anglers from the reservoirs. As I write this, I have before me a photograph of the famous trout anglers Bob Church and Peter Dobbs holding up two rainbow trout from Accrington Reservoir weighing 15½ lb and 11½ lb. Such sizes in Britain, even from reservoir fisheries, were unknown fifty years ago, and trout around this size were hailed as record fish, caught once in a lifetime. Today giant rainbows are quite common.

In Ireland in Lough Mask in County Mayo they still catch 'natural' brown trout of well over 5 lb, and Fred Wagstaffe once had three trout between 10 and 11 lb in one week, followed by a 13½ pounder later. And the late Bill Keal had one over 16 lb. Catches on this water have produced a trout of 18¾ pounds, and in 1977 a fish of 20 lb was caught by a French lady. So far as I can find out, no 'tricks' were used in getting these fish. All were caught on the fly, except the 18¾ pounder which took a lobworm. Indeed all the others were fished for using 'loch-style' methods with wet fly cast on the surface then retrieved in the usual way.

There's more than one way to catch your trout

When I first started fishing for trout many years ago, I thought that there was only one kind of trout, one kind of fishing and one sort of water in which they lived. I fished wet-fly on a river fifty yards from our weekend cottage, and that was that. Ignorance was bliss and my isolation in this fishing paradise lasted some years before I realized there were other places and other obsessions.

Since those halcyon days on the river bank at our cottage, of course, I have fished on many waters and in many areas and countries. The ice-fishers in North America who jiggle little rods through holes in the ice, while sitting back in armchairs inside little huts and smoking cigars, fascinated me almost as much as

Down to the river again for a day in Paradise!

the river rainbow trout anglers in Canada who forbid wet-fly fishing downstream.

The seatrout anglers in the Ythan estuary in Scotland, the dry-fly masters of the Ardennes in Belgium and the knee-padded tweedy purists of the Test in southern England have all expanded my experience with *Salmo trutta* to an extent I would never have believed when I was in the cocoon of my weekend hideaway those many years ago.

As you develop in your sport, become more curious and expand your game-fishing activities, you will inevitably come across other trout anglers whose activities you comprehend not. It may be that you will change jobs and move house away from an area whose waters you have known and loved for years. The river you have dry-flied every Saturday, the local reservoir where you and your friend had a boat regularly, the little hill lochs you fish from the banks — these familiar fishing holes may be only memories when you move to a new home.

If you want to lessen the pain of change, my advice to you as a trout angler is to adapt to the new waters that are available, as quickly as possible. If you have been an avid stillwater fisher and are now within striking distance of a good river, join a local club as early as possible, watch how others fish and change accordingly. Conversely, if you have been a chalk-stream dry-flier all your life and find yourself with no water but huge, featureless reservoirs within reach, learn all you can about shooting heads and Baby Dolls and stripping back.

Trout fishing is trout fishing certainly, but there are as many different ways of catching trout legally as there are types of water. And the methods used by anglers are usually dictated by the circumstances in which they are confined. It is quite senseless for one kind of trout angler to condemn another kind simply because they use a 'strange' method. I have no particular yen for fishing some of these 'concrete bowls', reservoirs in the London area which are stocked with rainbows and fished by anglers using big lures

and long-haul tactics. But I certainly don't let my prejudice get in the way of acknowledging their great advantages to a vast population of city anglers desperate for sport. Nor can I deny that some huge catches are made.

'There's more than one way to skin a cat' is an old saying, and in an angling sense, there is certainly more than one way of legally catching trout. So whether you are an upstream clearwater normer, a loch-style stillwater caster, or a knee-padded dry-fly purist, be tolerant of other anglers' methods of catching fish.

Trolling for monsters

Trolling for trout from a boat is certainly not a method of fishing which would be approved of by most anglers, and certainly *never* by the fly-fishers. Yet I have trolled for trout of a special kind on a Scottish Highland loch — the trout ferox, the really big fish that inhabits some of these mountain lochs. It is a fish which is plainly cannibal in its feeding habits, insect food no longer satisfies or nourishes it. Some of these fish grow to a weight of 10 lb or more.

Trolling is a method more widely used for salmon or grilse fishing. Indeed, on some lakes in America and Canada no other method is used. I have fished this way for Coho and Pacific salmon respectively in Lake Michigan and at Nanaimo off the British Columbia coast, and although we certainly caught plenty of fish, I found the whole business rather boring. Our rods were tackled up with Toby spoons and these were put over the stern of the boat and carried down very deeply by large ball weights. When a fish struck there was a quick-release mechanism which freed the weight and left the fish hooked for the angler to play and net. The weight was later recovered with a small electric winch.

Although I would find it difficult to imagine this method being used for trout, even lake trout, there is no doubt that trolling is the only acceptable method of fishing for these big ferox if you should find yourself on a loch that has them. For that reason, here is a brief description of the tackle and method of trolling (which is really another word for 'trawling').

Although you *can* troll in a boat using oars, it is a tiring job. The oarsman has to maintain a regular speed over a long period, and few oarsmen welcome the task. The practical way is to use an outboard engine. A slow, steady speed is required and indeed you can buy a special propellor for some outboards, which are made for trolling purposes.

A spinning rod is tackled up with nylon of a suitable breaking strain. If it is a ferox you are after, a breaking strain of 10 or

15 lb is advisable. The weight has to be of the kind the sea-anglers use to get the lure down deep. I have always found a silver or a gold Toby spoon best as a lure.

You start up the engine and let out about thirty or forty yards of nylon, keep a good grip on the handle of the rod, and wait as you troll to and fro for that powerful pull signifying that a fish has taken the spoon. Stop the engine, lift your rod and keep strain on the fish. In most cases you can be sure he is well hooked if he has been caught on the troll. The rest now is up to you and a good net.

Trout ferox are big fish and excellent fighters. Some anglers who fish these lochs where there are ferox will say that, like pike, they are better out of the water. They may be right, but don't imagine that by taking one of these monsters home, you have a fine fish for the table. As a rule, they do not cook well and the flesh tastes earthy.

Fish in comfort

It is nothing short of a howling gale. The wind is driving the rain almost horizontally in steely lines of stinging coldness on to your face and your numbed hands. The hat you are wearing is of tweed, certainly, but already it is sodden and useless as a head covering. The old waterproof jacket you wear is patently leaking at the shoulders, and in any case is too short to cover that part of your thighs between the tops of your waders and the edge of the jacket. This means that your upper thighs are already soaked. To make matters worse, those studded waders are leaking at the soles and you think that if somebody drove a big nail through your right leg you would hardly feel it!

You are miles from your car and on this particular reservoir there is no shelter. You decide to squelch on and hope for the best. Yet you know that 'the best' will only be when the rain stops; you are soaked anyway for the rest of the day. What is worse, you catch no fish.

This is a scenario I have written from personal experience. It happened to me only once, and that was enough to convince me never, never, never to skimp on, or neglect, first-class, top-of-the-league waterproof clothing. And that also means top and toe — hat and waders.

Think about this for a moment. An angler goes to rivers or lakes or reservoirs where, if he is lucky, there is the barest minimum of shelter if it rains, under trees or a rock. Usually there is nothing at all between him and the elements, except what he

Top *Near dam walls and structures are hot spots. This is Cod Beck reservoir in Yorkshire.*

Above *A Middlesex angler with his 18lb trout from Leighton Park Reservoir.*

is wearing. As a rule, he is miles from home and a long, long way from his car. The anglers who can carry on fishing doggedly (and often very successfully) through a downpour are those who are dry and tolerably warm inside their armour of good gear.

Waterproof clothing must be *total*. The tiniest unattended crack or opening can cause an angler dreadful discomfort in a rainstorm. Some of the new waxed waterproof jackets vary a great deal in quality and reliability, and I would advise anyone about to buy one, to buy the best. A jacket should be carefully inspected at least once a year and any creases showing signs of wear treated with the waxing substance supplied by reputable makers.

However vulnerable an angler may be fishing from the bank of a treeless stillwater when it rains, consider the situation on a boat. Waterproof trousers are essential here, simply because the seat gets wet, and wearing a rather short waterproof jacket and knee-high wellingtons is an ideal combination for having a cold, wet rear-end all day.

The most common opinion about fishing hats is that you will never catch a fish unless you are wearing a funny one. And by the looks of some anglers' headgear, they must catch a lot of fish! More seriously, a good fishing hat should be able to resist all the elements for a long, long time. It should have a brim sloping at the rear to prevent rain going down your neck. And the brim at the front should give some shielding for your eyes.

Although hats made entirely of waterproof material keep the rain off, they can be hot and very uncomfortable in good weather. The ideal hat is one which is a compromise between keeping the head at a moderate temperature and keeping the rain off for a long time. Some of the closely-knit tweed fore-and-aft jobs do this very well, as well as looking good when festooned with fishing flies!

Shun dogma

If angling for trout were a matter of logic and in the practical realms of most sports, with rules and certainties of behaviour, barely half the books on the subject would ever have been written. Indeed I doubt if the venerable 'grandfather' of angling literature, Izaak Walton himself, would have bothered to give advice through the many volumes of his works.

What makes this activity (is it a sport or an art?) so very different is the behaviour of the trout itself. Not even the salmon is so difficult to predict, although as many books giving advice are written about the king of fish. The trout and its vulnerability to being caught by an angler's wiles and lures is a subject for advice from almost everyone who has held a fishing rod in his hand. Don't do this, do that. Don't try that fly, try this one. Fish deep, fish on the surface.

My advice to beginners is simple: see all, hear all, dismiss a lot. As the years have gone by I have learned to read what other anglers write and to pay attention to what my own experience confirms, and to ignore what I feel will not work. And this is the suggestion I would make to others starting to fish.

When I meet some 'expert' who, I am told, 'has thirty years' experience' in fishing for trout, I ask myself, 'I wonder if he has thirty years' experience — *real* experience — or one year's experience multiplied thirty times?' There is a difference. I have known so-called angling experts who are still practising the methods they used years ago. And their dogmatic reasons range from 'Say what you like, angling's the same as it was years ago', to 'You can keep these new-fangled ideas. I'll stick to what I know for success.'

Before anglers realized that on stillwaters the depths at which fish were feeding was vitally important on a particular day, everyone used wet flies in the 'loch-style' manner — casting out and retrieving hour after hour, sometimes without the slightest sign of a fish. Then along came the 'long-line' anglers with their weight-forward lines and shooting heads and fancy lures. They experimented time and again and inevitably found their fish at the correct depths under certain conditions. Today, 'loch style' is still used widely, particularly on Scottish lochs, and in certain circumstances of wind and weather the method can be deadly in catching fish. But the point is that *other* methods were tried and tested by adventurous anglers, and found to be excellent.

Much of the sport — like the making of a Scotch malt whisky — is a mystery. One technique successful one day may be a dismal failure the next. This is not to say that the ignorant angler who simply 'chucks it and chances it' stands to get as many fish as the angler who studies the situation and fishes according to his best judgement. In fishing, like everything else, ignorance reaps its own poor harvest.

Without doubt, the knowledgeable angler is most likely to be the successful one. But how he becomes knowledgeable is to a large extent dependent on his own willingness to learn something new on every trip. He should be willing to experiment with new ideas and try out different flies, lures, lines, rods, reels and methods. More particularly he should never be book-bound or hidebound in the traditional methods that are given as certainties.

The angler fishes in a very uncertain world — the world of the trout.

Chapter 11

Other methods

Nymph fishing

You should know by this time that trout do not rely entirely for food on flies from the surface of the water. Indeed, surface-feeding is by no means their main dietary occupation. They feed on all kinds of insect — some from the bottom, some emerging from the bottom, some sinking to the bottom.

There are over 20,000 named British types of insect. Some are winged and some are not. There is one type of aquatic insect, an upwinged creature which develops under water, and at a certain stage is called a nymph. It is this stage that the angler tries to emulate with his artificial nymph flies. Apart from various Latin names which are difficult to recognize or remember, some of these types are called the Bottom Crawler, the Moss Creeper and the Stone Clinger, and there are many others.

Although the artificial nymph is used by dry-fly anglers, it is essential that it sinks. A nymph which floats as does the ordinary dry fly, is useless because the purpose of the nymph is to hook the fish *under* the surface. It need hardly be said, that if you are fishing with them the hooks must be absolutely rust free, and kept sharp.

There is one peculiarity about nymph fishing which will interest you. Unlike the artificial dry fly, the actual pattern of the nymph is less important than the way it is fished. Providing it really *is* an artificial nymph, keeping it lively and brisk in movement under the water is more important. And what is even *more* important is the depth at which it is fished. This may be anything from a few inches to some feet. And, of course, judging how far and exactly where it will sink to reach where the trout is feeding, requires considerable skill.

The rod, line and leader for nymph fishing is the same generally as used for dry-fly fishing. The line used must be a floater, because the more leisurely 'tightening-up' method of striking used with the dry fly simply will not do here. So far as the reel is concerned, there seems to be a good case here for using one of the comparatively recent automatic-retrieval type with the trigger placed just at your little finger. This kind of reel certainly strikes fast.

In case you are in any doubt at this stage about the effectiveness of nymph fishing, you will be interested to know that in some rivers and lakes fishing with nymph is allowed only after a certain date, perhaps in July when the trout are mostly going for surface flies.

When should you replace the dry fly with the artificial nymph, assuming that it is allowed on the water? Obviously, since the trout take the nymph under the surface, the time to use it is when there is no surface activity, yet you feel certain the fish are feeding under it. In the height of the season, trout are always feeding somewhere. On the other hand, if you see trout feeding on the surface, that is the time to offer them your artificial fly and forget the nymph.

It is easy to be fooled by trout in their feeding habits. This has happened to me, particularly on lakes in a dead-flat calm water. I have seen trout 'dimpling' all around the boat, yet they have shown not the slightest interest in anything wet or dry that I have offered. The reason is that these fish are taking nymphs just before they reach the surface. This is a very difficult stage of an insect's development to emulate. Dry flies will not do it. Wet flies are no good because they sink downwards from the surface. Well-placed and skilfully handled artificial nymphs are the only answer, so that instead of the trout fooling us, we can fool him.

Nymph fishing on a river can have its thrilling moments when you see no signs at all of surface activity. To all appearances the river is 'dead', yet you know only too well that the trout are feeding somewhere on *something*. This is the time to really 'read' the water and look, not for signs of rising fish, but for typical places where trout will almost certainly be lying. Deep holes at or near the far bank, holes behind rocks providing shelter for a fish from the fast current, clumps of weed or other growth providing the same kind of shelter.

This is when fishing with nymph comes into its own. You cast your nymph upstream of where you think the fish may be lying, and the place where it lands should have it sinking to the depth you feel is right. At this stage in clear water, you may even see signs of the fish moving towards your nymph. If and when your nymph disappears, strike at once.

Some interesting facts about trout with nymphs

Although I have no doubt at all that one or some of our experts in Britain have examined the trout's preference in food, the information on the subject which I have come across refers to the trout in New Zealand and Australia. And I can tell you that if what I have read is also relevant in other parts of the world, I am surprised that more anglers on rivers do not use artificial nymphs exclusively — especially the dry-fly anglers.

The famous angling expert and author E.M. Skues in 1938 wrote *Nymph fishing for chalk stream trout*, a book which is recognized today as exceptionally authoritative. In 1963, *Nymph fishing in practice* by Oliver Kite was published, followed by *Nymphs and the trout* by Frank Sawyer. So there has been no scarcity of information concerning the advantages of fishing with nymphs.

In 1952 some fishing experts in New Zealand made a study of the feeding habits of trout in the Horokiwi stream near Wellington. The study was conducted by Mr K. Radway Allen, and his report tells us that the main sources of food for trout are (i) the insect larvae and other small animals living among the stones and weeds of the bed of the stream; (ii) insects which come from the land and fall or are washed into the stream; (iii) small fish of various kinds.

Perhaps you knew all this, or had at least gathered it from what I have been saying in earlier parts of the book. What I did *not* know — and which may surprise you — was the proportions of these three kinds of food eaten by the trout. Although we can see with our own eyes that surface food is taken by the trout in summer, the study found that it is still only five per cent or less of the food which trout eat. And during the rest of the year it is rarely more than two per cent. Among the older trout the number of small fish found in the stomachs was quite few although, because of their size, they contributed 20 per cent to the trout's diet.

You see what this New Zealand study means? It means that by far the biggest good intake for trout is the insect life that comes from the *bottom* of the river. The experts reckoned it formed about 95 per cent of the weight of food eaten by the fish in their first two years of life, and about 75 per cent thereafter.

Although this study took place in New Zealand, statistics in Australian trout waters revealed the same trend. *Fly fishing in Australia and New Zealand* by M.E. McCausland showed an analysis of stomach contents of rainbow trout from a river in New South Wales. He found the same situation regarding trout preferences in food.

An angler is into a hefty trout on Leighton Reservoir, Yorkshire.

Some American angling writers support these studies and say
that in the USA a diet of nymphs is three-quarters of a trout's diet.
In Britain the same conclusions are reached by eminent writers
such as Dr W.E. Frost and Dr M.E. Brown.

Nymphs, therefore, are the trout's staple diet, and it is surprising that not more trout anglers recognize this and fish the
artificial varieties, instead of somewhat slavishly casting their wet
and dry flies. Certainly wet flies sink on their downstream journey but, let's face it, they make no pretence of trying to deceive
the trout into believing they are bottom-sourced insects. Surface
flies that gradually sink represent no more than 20 per cent of
the trout's diet.

Fishing with worm

There is much controversy about bait fishing for trout. At one end
of the argument are the fly 'purists', who say that the use of a
worm or a maggot is outrageous, that it doesn't give the fish a
sporting chance. At the other end are the wormers who contend
that bait fishing is not all that easy, that for instance upstream clearwater worming is indeed an art and, in any case, as few fish are
caught on a worm as on a fly.

Trout feed eagerly on worm in flood
water.   *A Stewart tackle baited with worm.*

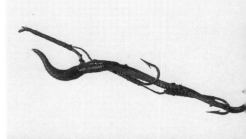

Depending on your own sporting tastes, the rules of any club you may join, and the regulations on the water you fish, you must make up your own mind about this. For my part, I have had as much sporting fun from using a worm under certain conditions as casting a fly.

It should be said that fishing for trout with a worm can be very effective, especially when the river is full or in spate. Trout feed on worm and other insects in a flood water, and eagerly snatch a juicy morsel streaming past.

If you fish with worm, make sure that your nylon leader is weighted with small shot, as many of them as are needed to get the bait down, yet not *too* far down, and make it drift downstream at a natural-looking pace. This is a trial-and-error business.

On a single hook the worm should simply be impaled. On a Stewart Tackle (three hooks in a row) the worm should be arranged so that *all* the hooks are concealed, so far as possible.

Some people fish with worm using a bubble-float to keep the bait at a prescribed depth in a slow-moving water, but I have no experience of this. Nor, I fancy, would it attract me.

I have often had good sport fishing the worm upstream in small burns and moorland streams. The ideal place to do this is where there is a good head of white water rushing into a fairly deep pool. That's where the trout are lying, often some surprisingly large ones of a pound or more, and angling in places like this with a worm is more like stalking or hunting than fishing.

Here is what you do. Approach the stream very cautiously, and keep well back from the bank. Then get down on one knee and simply get the lie of the land for a while. Stay still. Face upstream towards the waterfall or rough water. Quietly and slowly peel off some line from your reel and, assuming your hook is baited with a worm, cast it right into the white water.

Now, this is not easy. You are not casting a fly, and a hooked worm is heavier, more cumbersome to cast. Nevertheless, after two or three attempts you should be able to get the worm where you want it to be — in the middle of the rough torrent.

Immediately raise your rod and get your nylon leader free of the water, so that it is only your hooked worm which is travelling down with the stream. If a trout takes it, you will be under no doubt. Raise the point of your rod and tighten your line with your left hand. He's on. The rest is up to your angling skill.

Worm fishers have all sorts of peculiar ideas about how to treat their bait, mainly to toughen them so that they will stay on the hook. Frankly, I have little time for the 'toughening up' methods, because if a worm does not stay on your hook, perhaps it is time you took a second look at how you cast it! Once I have dug up

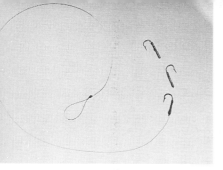

The Stewart tackle.

Fresh moss keeps the worms clean and lively.

a few worms of the size I feel suits my hook, I put them in a little perforated plastic bait box (the tacklists sell them) then put in some fresh moss. This keeps the worms clean and lively.

Fishing the worm downstream in a current requires a lot of trial-and-error skill and judgement involving the depth of the water, the speed of the current and the ideal rate at which the worm is travelling, so that it appears to the fish that a natural tit-bit has been carried down to it. The worm ideally should simply tumble down. If the current is strong, you have to add a few more shot weights to prevent the worm simply riding on the surface and therefore over the fish's heads. If you have too *much* weight, it will stick on the bottom too often. The skill is in getting the best balance between these factors.

There are two kinds of hook you can use for worm fishing. The first is the ordinary single hook, usually 12 or 14 for trout fishing. You simply impale the worm on to this hook, and even if the point of the hook shows, don't worry too much about it because, in my experience at any rate, the trout are not put off by this. The second type of hook is the Stewart Tackle, which is really three hooks in sequence which are intended to hold the worm firmly and naturally. I can affirm the benefits of the former but have doubts about the latter. Frankly, I prefer the single hook because it does not get stuck on the bottom so often as the Stewart.

Once you have cast your worm into the current, even although you have the depth of water and the speed of the current judged accurately, you simply cannot permit your bait to drift down as the current takes it. You must keep in constant 'telegraphic' touch with the worm. Keep your rod up and with your non-casting hand hold the line so that you can feel how your worm is handling. Do everything gently and smoothly, and if a trout *does* take your worm, raise your rod further, and gently but firmly tighten on the line.

When you are casting over towards the opposite bank of the river, don't worry too much if you overshoot the water and your worm lands on the bank. Depending on where it lands, of course, this *may* mean the loss of your hook and leader, but in most cases you will be able to get it off the bank gently and see it flop into the water. This is excellent if and when it happens, because the worm is then being carried in the current very close to the bank and that is often where a big trout is lying in wait for just such a morsel to pass.

Fishing with a worm on a river calls for a thorough covering of all the water. This means that every stream has to be explored with great stealth and the worm, by careful casting, allowed to drift downstream in the most natural manner possible. Wade very softly and 'read' the river before you cast. Look for every likely lie in which you feel the trout is feeding with minimum effort and maximum potential.

The time that brings out wormers galore is when the river is coming down in a brown-coloured spate. Most of them in my opinion are chuck-it-and-chance-it fishers who simply throw their baited hooks into the water and hope for the best.

Take my advice — don't join them. Worm fishing is a skill, and a river in flood provides a fine challenge for that skill. Fish which might take up a good feeding spot when the river is running normally are nowhere near these spots during a spate. The reason is obvious; they get out of the way of the fast-moving flood. Where do they go? Well, where would *you* go if you were a trout? That's right – into the bank, even under it, and behind sheltering rocks.

Look for these places. In many cases trout are lying just a foot or so off the bank from which you are fishing. In a spate it is surprising how near fish can be, unsuspecting and unsuspected. Flood water hides you, hides the fish, and can even conceal your worm, unless it is trundled quite slowly past the fish's nose! This means using a little more weight on the leader to slow it down. It also means searching out those calmer eddies just off the main current where fish could be lying, virtually 'sheltering from the storm'.

Spinning for trout

Spinning? For *trout*? Outrageous! Scandalous! *That's* not sporting.

I can well imagine some 'purists' revolted at the idea of using a spinning rod and artificial minnows or spoons to catch the noble brown trout. Indeed I know very well that this method would be expressly forbidden on many trout waters. For seatrout — perhaps. But not brown trout.

I make no particular plea for the method. To me, trout fishing is mainly fly fishing, but I do realize that many anglers get a lot of good sport from catching trout using a spinning rod and — this is important — many of the bigger fish that are 'cannibals' and eat smaller trout can only be caught this way, and are perhaps better out of the water anyway, especially in stillwaters where restocking is an expensive business.

Let me explain first what spinning is. The spinning rod and reel is a different tackle altogether from your fly rod and reel. The rod is shorter (although some sea-fishing and salmon-fishing spinning rods are all of ten to twelve feet), and the method of fishing is quite different. The reel is really a winding-on business with a baler which neatly winds the nylon line on to a fixed spool.

The lure you use is an imitation minnow, usually called a Devon, or a spoon, which is almost exactly what it is called — like a tablespoon without the handle — or any combination of these. The fishing tackle shops sell these spinning lures in all sorts of shapes, sizes and colours — flashing things that wobble under the water, twittering things that spin round and round, wobbling things that behave like a wounded small fish. The variety is nearly endless.

You fasten your lure to the end of your nylon line. It is usually heavy enough to be cast out and retrieved at the correct depth of water, but, if not, you can add lead shot weights anywhere on the line to get is sunk deeper. Then you can put your finger on th fixed spool of your reed to hold the nylon line when you unfasten the baler. You are now ready to cast.

As the nylon line is now quite free, when you cast out the line will strip off until your lure plops into the water, perhaps twenty or thirty yards out from the bank. Then you simply wind the handle and the baler automatically springs into action, retrieving your line and your lure. The lure spins or wobbles under the surface possibly imitating a small fish or some other creature, and hopefully attracting one of those bigger trout to the treble hook on its tail.

A word about swivels. As you will appreciate, the constant action of the imitation minnow spinning round and round reacts on the line itself, and unless this is counteracted in some way you may find yourself with a line horribly 'kinked', making further casting very difficult. There was a time when tackle shops sold left-hand spinning devons and right-hand ones so that the angler could change his minnow and avoid kinking, but the development of the ball-bearing swivel has modernized all this. This tiny swivel is very easy to fasten between the lure itself and the line, and it is quite essential for avoiding kinked lines.

There is another important piece of 'machinery' on your spinning reel, which you should learn to manipulate expertly. Spin-

Top left *A Toby lure for spinning.*

Top *a swivel for spinning lures.*

Above left *A spinning reel.*

Above *Shot weights.*

Left *A two-piece spinning rod.*

ning reels have a clutch, usually handily controlled by a little dial right at the front of the reel. The purpose of this is to impart to the line just the right amount of strain to enable the fish to be played and tired without reaching the breaking strain of the line. If you set your clutch too loosely (anti-clockwise) and a fish takes your lure, you could find your line being pulled and stripped off without restraint. If you set it too tightly (clockwise) and a big fish takes you, he will simply heave and pull until your rod is bent over and the inevitable happens — the line snaps.

Handling your clutch is a delicate business but you will soon get the hang of it. It is really a matter of compromise between the size of the fish you have on, the breaking strain of the nylon, and your ability to keep him fighting between these two factors.

Chapter 12

Home and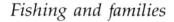

away

Fishing and families

Fishing for trout and keeping reasonable relations with your family is something at which you have to work, for anglers both male and female. (A lot of people forget that in Britain, at any rate, one in eight anglers is a woman.)

The ideal answer, of course, is simply for everyone in the family to go on the fishing trip together. The non-fishers can enjoy themselves doing all sorts of 'country' things like bird-watching or photographing, or just enjoying the environment. This is not always practical, however, as different ages and tastes will often clash with the trout angler's interests.

For my part, I never have any problem with my fishing trips, as my wife enjoys the countryside, enjoys being beside the water — river or lake — and relaxes in the car with a book or walks our dog. She has often said that were it not for my fishing trips, there would be no other reason to visit exceptionally beautiful parts of a river or picnic beside a beautiful lake. My fishing, she says, takes us to 'unexplored' territories. Frankly, I consider myself lucky for having such co-operation, and I know she is exceptional in her outlook.

It is another matter altogether for a man who is mad keen on angling, whose wife complains about his too-frequent absences from the home. Home repairs get neglected, their garden is often uncared for and, in extreme cases, his wife occasionally has to introduce him to the children! Fair's fair. Obsessive angling to this extent creates 'angling widows' and domestic friction.

One answer to this problem is for the angler to join a club and confine his fishing strictly to the dates of the club outings. This way he can plan his trips in advance, give his wife and family

Children love fishing — specially with Dad.

plenty of notice, and everyone knows where they stand. 'Club' day is Dad's Day, and nobody expects him home till late with, hopefully, a good string of fish.

Another palliative to the angling husband problem is for Dad to take one of the children with him on outings, providing they are of a suitable age, for safety reasons, and assuming that the child shows some signs of being keen to learn about fishing. This father-and-child fishing relationship can become a very reward-ing one, and it is amazing how many trout anglers you meet today who will tell you that their first taste for the sport came from a few fishing trips with their father.

A word of warning: *don't* agree to take anyone else's child fish-ing with you. The risks are too high, particularly in a boat on a lake. You can never tell in advance how someone else's little cherub may behave. He or she may jump around all over the place and endanger everyone's lives. I have a strict rule about this. My answer to anyone who asks me to take their child fishing is, 'Certainly — providing you come with us and look after the child.' That is usually the last I hear of the matter.

Fishing holidays are another problem to be solved. Some wives and families readily agree to going to a fishing hotel, or to an area that has good fishing, and some even agree to a week at one of these hotels which offer tuition for the whole family. Anglers with families like that are fortunate.

Other fishing husbands have to seek other remedies. And the best one I know on a 'fair shares' basis is for the angler to book into a fishing hotel for a week in addition to the annual family holiday. There is no other answer for the enthusiast.

Fishing with Dad

Father-and-son fishing is so popularly regarded in Canada and America that special Dads-and-kids weekend outings are organized by schools, churches and social groups. It is surprising that the notion has not caught on to the same extent in Britain and other European countries. In Britain there are an estimated 3½ million anglers of all kinds — coarse, game and sea fishers — and a large number of these attribute their enthusiasm for the sport to the encouragement they got from their father.

It can be a very rewarding rapport. The idea of getting up early and setting off with Dad to fish a river or a lake is exciting for the youngster, satisfying for the father because he has the feeling of responsible, caring parenthood, and pleasing to Mum because it is one less responsibility for her to worry about that day. And what warmer glow can there be on the face of *any* child than the one you see when he brings home his first fish for Mum to cook for breakfast!

Of all the kinds of fishing most suitable for father and son, angling for trout heads the list in my opinion. Coarse fishing may be fun enough for experienced competition men lining a river bank under umbrellas, and ground-baiting their 'swim' with hemp-seed or maggots. But what does little Brian do while Dad has one eye glued to that float and the other on his nearby competitor's keepnet? Sea fishing with a group out in a chartered boat, you have to be out on the briny all day to make the trip worth while. So what can little Brian do if he feels seasick twenty miles from shore? And, let's face it, father and son fishing from rocks and casting bait into a roaring sea is downright dangerous. Both going out in a small dinghy has its hazards, too, as we can see from newspaper reports every other week in summer.

The ideal fishing trip for Dad and his offspring is a trout trip. A river can be the best possible living 'blackboard' on which to write nature's many messages, illustrating the flora and fauna of the waterside at hand, pointing out the behaviour of various birds and animals, describing the plants and flowers, then describing the insect life, the batches of various flies, leading on naturally to the reality of fly fishing. And for the child it can be an experience which he will carry in his mind as one of childhood's fondest memories — a day on the river with Dad.

Salmon fishing creates another kind of atmosphere altogether. It's the Big League. Salmon beats on rivers are scarce and expensive, and who can blame even the fondest father if his mind is occupied every hour with catching the king of fish in order to make his expensive day worth while? Moreover, a 14-foot salmon fly rod is hardly the most suitable thing in the world with which to introduce a youngster to the glories of fishing!

Trout fishing is in my opinion the easiest, most suitable entrance-way for a child to the world of angling. All he needs is an inexpensive two-piece glass-fibre rod, a reel, a line, leader and flies and he is ready to assimilate every golden word from the most highly respected expert in the world — his Dad.

Armchair fishing

Some mention should be made about fishing from an armchair. By this I mean reading about the sport, especially in winter evenings. Some anglers spend a lot of time, money and eyesight avidly devouring all kinds of printed matter on the subject, and now that we are in the age of video, recorded tapes on angling are very popular in fishing clubs.

Collecting old books on angling is a pursuit in itself. If you go through the classified columns of angling magazines you will find there are people selling, buying and collecting old and rare books. With some anglers it is a fetish, and many public libraries are bequeathed large collections left by anglers who have passed on to fish ethereal waters.

There are hundreds and hundreds of books on the subject, ranging from Izaak Walton's *The Compleat Angler,* right up to today's brightly illustrated titles with exciting diagrams and colour pictures of stillwater fishers holding up trout enormously bigger than many older anglers ever dreamed about.

It is a good hobby and I would heartily recommend it for anglers in the off-season who have a yen for collecting.

Take the brochures with a pinch of salt!

Sooner or later you will want to experience fresh fishing fields in other countries. You may be lucky enough to get a few days' fishing while on a business trip thousands of miles from home; or you may have a really co-operative family who will allow you to fish some strange water while on holiday abroad.

Of course, once you know you are going on a trip like this, the first thing you will do is get hold of a brochure describing the fishing in the area. You will write to the tourist office and they will send you a fancy one in colour showing on the cover an angler fighting a huge fish. And you will be tempted to devour and believe every single word of the persuasive descriptions of the excellent fishing available, etc.

Not for worlds would I attempt to denigrate the world-famous fishing rivers and lakes of New Zealand (which I have never visited) or the teaming waters of Western Canada (which I *have* visited). More widely travelled and experienced trout anglers than I have written scores of books extolling the fishing in remote areas of all continents of the world (although, strangely, I have never come across any writing on angling in the USSR). I will say this, however: on such fishing trips that I have experienced in other countries, I found problems never even hinted at in the brochures. Conversely, I found benefits similarly neglected by the publicity people.

It may be different now, but years ago, in spite of the glowing boasts in the brochures, access to trout fishing in Czechoslovakia was almost impossible for a visitor. Why? Because it was all controlled by the Czech trade unions and they did not particularly welcome any strangers. I tried for five days to get a permit to fish and ended up on an unattractive, remote river that was apparently fishless.

In Canada you never read about the danger from bears in the brochures that describe the best fishing areas. Nor do they say anything about the black flies and mosquitoes that can ruin any trip. Conversely, I had never read about or even heard about the glorious trout fishing on the Bow River just a few miles downstream from Calgary. Some widely experienced anglers say it is the finest brown trout river in the world!

In Yugoslavia not one person in the area of Kranska Gora near the Austrian border could give me the slightest information about the excellent trout fishing available.

In the USA the distances to be travelled to reach trout waters are formidable, and most of the waters are well away from the popular 'brochure' holiday spots.

In France I found that hunting for fishing took ten times longer than fishing for trout.

In Denmark I found barren waters. In Germany's Harz Mountains the tourist people in Bad Harzburg seemed to be totally ignorant of any fishing available. Then I found that most of the area — and the fishing — was in the ownership of East Germany, and access was impossible.

Good fishing friends have brought back to me some hair-raising tales of fishing outside Britain. In the Austrian Tyrol, for instance, your guide throws your catch into a barrel which is strapped to his back for which privilege he charges very highly. In Bulgaria the tortuous process of getting a fishing permit takes days. And in Italy, in my experience, I do not believe they have seen a native trout in a century!

If you are thinking of fishing in a country other than your own, by all means have a go. But don't believe all you read in the

brochures. Make arrangements well in advance and hire a guide from a reputable fishing trip organization.

Read all about it!

It was an angling writer Cunliffe R. Pearce who said, 'A trout fisher should always be asking questions.' I totally agree with this, but I must say that the place to ask the questions and possibly find the answers is not always on the river or the lake. Sometimes the place to pose questions and find answers is between the covers of a good, authoritative angling book.

Some books on fishing are evergreens, classics of their type. Others come and go and possibly are never heard of again. What is remarkable is the sheer volume of books on the subject of angling. Only recently I obtained a listing of such books published in Britain alone, and it amounted to over a hundred currently in print. In connection with research on another work, I visited the Mitchell Library in Glasgow and was kindly given access to their books on sports fishing through many years of publication. That collection consisted of hundreds of volumes.

The problem therefore for a beginner in the sport is in knowing which books might be worthwhile in his education and which not. Izaak Walton's *The Compleat Angler*, of course, is probably one of the oldest and best-known books on the subject, and for those who might like to see how little has really changed in fishing for trout, this one will serve well.

Other books, many of them classics (available through your local library if not in print), which I would recommend as worth reading are:

> *Silk, Fur and Feather* by G.K.M. Skues
> *Fifty Popular Flies* by Ian Stuart (Benn) (3 volumes)
> *A Dictionary of Trout Flies* by A. Courtney Williams (Black) 1973
> *Trout and Nymphs* by Tony Orman (Hodder & Stoughton) 1974
> *Trout Flies — Natural and Artificial* by C.F. Walker (Herbert Jenkins) 1965
> *Trout Fly Recognition* by John Goddard (Black) 1971
> *A River Never Sleeps* by Roderick Haig-Brown (Collins) 1948
> *The Trout* by W.E. Frost and M.E. Brown (Collins) 1967
> *Nymphs and the Trout* by Frank Sawyer (Black) 1970
> *Nymph Fishing in Practice* by Oliver Kite (Barrie and Jenkins) 1963

A Fly Fisher's Life by Charles Ritz (Reinhardt) 1955

Guide to Trout Angling edited by Roger Hungerford (Pollard) 1971

The Practical Fly Fisherman by A.J. McClane (Prentice Hall) 1953

Stillwater Fly Fishing for Young People by Sidney du Broff (Kay and Ward, Kingswood) 1982

Catching Fish by Richard Walker (David & Charles) 1981

Reservoir Trout Fishing by Bob Church, 1983

A Complete Guide to Fishing (Marshall Cavendish Ltd) 1977

Trout — how to catch them edited by Kenneth Mansfield (Barrie and Jenkins Ltd) 1970

Flyfishing by Brian Furzer (Ward Lock Ltd) 1980

Trout Flies on Stillwater by John Goddard (A & C Black) 1972

Index